MW00611945

# HOW MUCH MORE

*DISCOVERING GOD'S*
*EXTRAVAGANT LOVE IN*
*UNEXPECTED PLACES*

## LISA HARPER

Lifeway Press®
Brentwood, Tennessee

Published by Lifeway Press®
© 2023 Lisa Harper

ISBN: 978-1-0877-7392-6
Item: 005839462
Dewey decimal classification: 231.7
Subject heading:  GOD / LOVE / KINDNESS

To order additional copies of this resource, write Lifeway Resources Customer Service; 200 Powell Place, Suite 100, Brentwood, TN 37027-7707; Fax order to 615.251.5933; call toll-free 800.458.2772; email orderentry@lifeway.com; or order online at lifeway.com.

Printed in the United States.

Lifeway Resources
200 Powell Place, Suite 100, Brentwood, TN 37027-7707

## EDITORIAL TEAM, LIFEWAY WOMEN BIBLE STUDIES

*Becky Loyd*
Director, Lifeway Women

*Tina Boesch*
Manager

*Sarah Doss*
Publishing Team Leader

*Mike Wakefield*
Content Editor

*Emily Chadwell*
Production Editor

*Chelsea Waack*
Graphic Designer

*Lauren Ervin*
Cover Design

# Table of Contents

# About the Author

Rarely are the terms "hilarious storyteller" and "theological scholar" used in the same sentence, much less used to describe the same person. But then again, Lisa Harper is anything but stereotypical! She's been lauded as a gifted communicator whose writing and speaking overflow with colorful pop culture references that connect the dots between the Bible era and modern life. Her style combines sound scriptural exposition with easy to relate to anecdotes and comedic wit.

Best-selling author and pastor Max Lucado calls Lisa one of the "best Bible tour guides around," and author Priscilla Evans Shirer adds, "Her God-given ability to not merely teach the Word but package it in a way that stirs the heart and calls to action is incomparable. When she speaks, ears perk up!"

Lisa's vocational resume includes thirty-plus years of vocational church and parachurch ministry leadership, including six years as the director of Focus on the Family's national women's ministry, where she created the popular Renewing the Heart conferences attended by almost two hundred thousand women. Her academic resume includes a Master of Theological Studies with honors from Covenant Seminary, and she is currently working on her doctorate at Denver Seminary.

Now a sought-after Bible teacher and speaker, she's been featured on numerous television and radio programs and is a regular on TBN's globally syndicated *Better Together* show. She's spoken at hundreds of national and international women's events, as well as in churches around the world. But she's also very invested locally and has been leading a weekly neighborhood Bible study for many years.

If you can't find Lisa studying, teaching, or riding a motorcycle, she's probably typing on a keyboard somewhere, because she's had fourteen books published, including the recent devotional, *LIFE: An Obsessively Grateful, Undone by Jesus, Genuinely Happy, and Not Faking It Through the Hard Stuff Kind of 100-Day*

*Devotional*, and has written and filmed five best-selling Bible study video curriculums, including *Job: A Story of Unlikely Joy*.

Yet when asked about her credentials, the most noticeable thing about Lisa is her authenticity. During a recent interview, she said, "I'm so grateful for the opportunities God's given me, but don't forget, He often uses donkeys and rocks!" She went on to describe her greatest accomplishment to date as getting to be Missy's mama. Because in April 2014, after a difficult two-year journey and several adoption losses, she finally got to bring her little girl home from Haiti, and she's been smiling ever since.

# Dedication

This study is dedicated to the leadership team and faculty at Denver Seminary, where my heart and mind have grown in gratitude and amazement over the extravagant, redemptive nature of God's love. I'm particularly thankful for the tutelage of Dr. Craig Blomberg, Dr. Lynn Cohick (now at Northern Seminary), Dr. Jim Howard, Dr. Don Payne, and Dr. Marshall Shelley, all of whom have brilliantly, graciously, and patiently "scootched" me further into the embrace of our Creator Redeemer and encouraged me to dive ever deeper into His Word. Anything I've spoken or written in *How Much More* that sounds wise or spiritually astute was surely paraphrased from one of their books, lectures, or a conversation in which I peppered them with questions!

# How Much More

Remember the Sabbath day, to keep it holy: You are to labor six days and do all your work, but the seventh day is a Sabbath to the LORD your God. You must not do any work—you, your son or daughter, your male or female servant, your livestock, or the resident alien who is within your city gates. For the LORD made the heavens and the earth, the sea, and everything in them in six days; then he rested on the seventh day. Therefore the LORD blessed the Sabbath day and declared it holy.

## EXODUS 20:8-11

The LORD spoke to Moses: "Speak to the Israelites and tell them: These are my appointed times, the times of the LORD that you will proclaim as sacred assemblies. 'Work may be done for six days, but on the seventh day there is to be a Sabbath of complete rest, a sacred assembly. You are not to do any work; it is a Sabbath to the LORD wherever you live.'"

## LEVITICUS 23:1-3

## Session One: THE HEART BEHIND THE HERDING

julie    951 751 0684

## DISCUSSION QUESTIONS

What impacted you the most from the video teaching?

Lisa said that God always has been and always will be working on our behalf. Do you really believe that? If so, why? If not, share a bit about your struggle.

How would you define *imago Dei* to a friend who doesn't know much about God or Christianity? Why is this such an important truth?

How do you see the redemptive heart of God in His "herding" Adam and Eve out of the garden of Eden? How have you experienced God's redemptive heart in times He has herded you?

How have you seen God take what some would see as the least and use it mightily for His purposes and glory?

When you look back on your story, how have you experienced the goodness and kindness of God in all your circumstances?

How did this video teaching reveal the redemptive heart and extravagant love of God?

Knock, knock.

Who's there?

Interrupting cow.

Interrupting cow, who?

Mooooooooooo!

That was my daughter, Missy's, favorite joke when she was four years old and first learning English. (I became a mom through the miracle of adoption, and Missy is originally from Haiti.) She'd usually erupt into giggles before she even got to the moo part, which then gave her the cutest kind of *carte blanche* to go back to the beginning and start the joke all over again. Of course, by the third or fourth round of the knock-knock joke, we'd both be so tickled it didn't matter whether she got to the end or not. Simply watching Missy's brown eyes twinkle when she said, "Hey, Mama, knock, knock!" and listening to her lovely Creole accent when she did her best to pronounce "interrupting" was enough to make my heart swell with affection. In light of everything my little girl had to endure and overcome after her first mom died when Missy was a baby, just seeing her alive is enough for me. But whenever my kid excels at something like doing cannon-balls into the pool or multiplying fractions, well, you'd better shut the front door, baby, because this mama will absolutely commence happy dancing—preferably holding a huge neon sign that says, "That's my girl!"

I've been a follower of Christ since I was itty-bitty, and now I'm oldy-goldy, which means I've known Jesus for more than half a century. Plus, I grew up in a very conservative family and church culture and have been in vocational ministry for over thirty years. I'm pretty sure I've been exposed to all the Bible stories in some setting or another—Sunday School, Vacation Bible School, Christian summer camp, youth group, worship services, seminary, revivals, women's conferences, small group Bible studies, large group Bible studies, and so forth. But it wasn't until I experienced what felt like a seismic shift in my heart several years ago, when I began a doctoral candidacy at Denver Seminary, that I began to actually imagine our holy, trinitarian God belly laughing alongside me, thoroughly delighted that I'm His daughter and pleased as punch that I'm learning new things.

Our fervent prayer is that *How Much More* will help you experience a fresh, enlarged awareness of God's delight in you too. We have audacious hope that this study will help you clearly recognize God's consistent and redemptive grace from cover to cover of the Bible—from the creation in Genesis to the scriptural caboose of Revelation. Because, despite common assumption, there aren't any "bad" chapters in God's story.

> Describe a time when you felt bowled over (in the redemptive sense, of course!) by a Spirit-generated juggernaut of comprehension. What "fresh" truth has God's Spirit revealed to you recently?

*1. The time I was filled w/ Spirit of God after praying with Bill. it was pure love.*

*2. The fresh truth everyday that I am a sinner but God loves me anyways!*

> Read 1 John 1:5. How would you paraphrase this verse in your own words? Is there a secret corner of your heart that figuratively crosses its arms and cocks an eyebrow suspiciously at John's proclamation? If so, why?

*Not at all! God is light and darkness will never overcome it even though it tries really hard to - all the time. Even in the darkest times I have learned to look for even the faintest glimmer of light because that is where God is.*

John said, "There is absolutely no darkness in Him." Really? Perhaps when you read that declaration you quickly agree, but then you think of some passages in Scripture that sure sound kind of dark, or at least feel that way. Maybe it causes you to wonder about God's character. Maybe a shadow of doubt falls over your belief that God is absolutely for you. To still the wonder and chase the shadow, we're going to tackle some of those passages over the next few weeks. In the end we will verify what John said and confirm the following truth I've discovered:

Our Creator and Redeemer has always been and—until He calls us home to be with Him in glory—will always be in the process of restoring the dignity and value He has built into us, His beloved image bearers!

## The How of "How Much More"

I've often teased my counselor, Lynn, about being her job security. She has been such a means of grace that I can't imagine navigating some of the more difficult seasons and relationships in my life without her. She's shared a plethora of wisdom with me over the years, and, because my heart often lags behind my head, she kindly puts much of it in analogous form so I'm not tempted to overanalyze it and miss the main point. One of my favorite analogies from her reframed my view of change. I was in the middle of trying to reform some really unhealthy behaviors I'd foolishly repeated in several friendships and dating relationships, and my attempts weren't being well received, especially by a few dear long-term friends. When I described the pushback and resistance I was getting, Lynn said that changing ingrained patterns—even unhealthy or sinful ones—was much like changing a dance style in the middle of a song. For instance, "dance partners" (i.e., friends, family members, a spouse, and so forth) get used to our particular "relational choreography," so changing our steps from a waltz to a foxtrot smack-dab in the middle of a routine they have memorized totally throws them off-balance. It takes a lot of time and effort to learn a new dance style, and some would rather not go through that awkward, toe-crushing season when they already have another routine down pat, even if it's unhealthy.

I couldn't help but think of that analogy when I was in the early stages of praying about and planning for this project. For many of us, understanding *how much more* God loves us and is actively working on our behalf is going to require changing some presumptions we have about Scripture, as well as changing some of the steps we've grown accustomed to when it comes to engaging the biblical text. This new dance might get a little uncomfortable. We might break out into a sweat, and we'll probably get our toes stepped on a time or two, but it will be so very worth it in the end. Through the guidance of God's Spirit and the revelation of His Word, I believe we'll have increased security in His love, increased desire to know and commune with Him through Scripture, and increased passion to share the living hope of Jesus Christ in tangible ways in order to help redeem the world around us.

So here's the new four-step pattern we're going to practice together:

**Stretching Sacred Muscles**

**Learning Redemptive Rhythms**

**Following God's Lead**

**Dancing For Good**

And to help these four steps sink in, we're going to connect them with four spiritual disciplines. If you're an Enneagram One, someone who prefers routine, or are simply used to Bible studies with prescribed daily "homework" sections, please feel free to complete one of these disciplines per day of the week. Since there are four sections instead of five, you'll have one whole weekday left over for review! But if you're more like me and typically don't have the same schedule each week, then complete these sections/spiritual dance steps as you have time. Frankly, some of my best Bible study moments are when the rest of my house is asleep.

Here's how we're going to get into the *how much more* flow:

**STRETCHING SACRED MUSCLES** will help us *peruse* God's Word. The definition of *peruse* is "to examine or consider with attention and in detail."[1] Acts 17:11 says the Bereans "received the word with eagerness and examined the Scriptures daily to see if these things were so." Just like those ancient Bereans, we want to dig into God's promises to get a better understanding of who we are as His beloveds and how to lean more fully into an intimate relationship with Him.

**LEARNING REDEMPTIVE RHYTHMS** will help us pause to *ponder* what we've read and examined. Well-seasoned (pun intended) barbecue chefs—or "pit masters"—say that the tastiest, tenderest meat has been allowed to marinate for a long time. So it is with followers of Christ. It takes a while for the truth of God's Word to permeate our hearts and tenderize those places where the difficulties and disappointments of life have built up callouses of skepticism or self-protection. Dutifully studying the Bible, in and of itself, doesn't necessarily equate with delighting in God, much less resting in His delight for us. Taking the time to really marinate in the awesome truths revealed in Scripture is what pays the highest spiritual dividends. As the psalmist wrote, "How happy is the one" whose "delight is in the LORD's instruction, and he meditates on it day and night" (Ps. 1:1,2).

**FOLLOWING GOD'S LEAD** will help us establish the habit of both *praying* about what we're learning and *praying* God's promises deeper into our hearts. From the beginning of biblical history, it's clear that God wanted an intimate relationship with us, not some superficial transactional relationship where we just ask Him for stuff and He gives it to us based on merit or whim. We don't have to walk around afraid that He's going to whack us over the head when we misbehave, make a wrong choice, or say a word that's not in the Bible when we're stuck in bad traffic (mind you, I'm simply hypothesizing at this point!). And the foundation of real, intimate relationships is good communication, which is surely why Paul encouraged the Colossians, "Devote yourselves to prayer; stay alert in it with thanksgiving" (Col. 4:2).

And finally, **DANCING FOR GOOD** will help us put what we're learning into **PRAXIS**, which may just sound like a fancy term for "practice," yet there's actually a significant difference between the two words. Unlike *practice*, which can describe rote behavior like practicing one's multiplication tables or parallel parking skills, **PRAXIS** refers to an action in which there is inherent meaning that reflects the motive of one's heart. (Watch for words marked like **PRAXIS** throughout the study. You'll find more information on these words in our Weighty Words section at the end of each week.) The bottom line is, God calls us not to simply study His Word to increase our head knowledge but to actually "flesh out" biblical truths in light of the transformation that has taken place in our hearts. As James encouraged Christians, "Be doers of the word and not hearers only" (Jas. 1:22a).

Of course, learning a new spiritual dance style is going to take a little time, y'all. So take a couple of deep breaths, freshen up your coffee (or electrolyte enhanced "smart" water for those of you super healthy gluten-free types who are surely clad in yoga pants), and let's get started!

# Stretching Sacred Muscles

The first images that used to race through my mind when I heard the word *Sabbath* were of prudish bathing suits and push mowers. You see, when I was growing up, my mom was emphatic about keeping the Sabbath holy. (Scripture basically defines Sabbath as a day of abstention from secular work that follows each six-day working week.)[2] And for a Southern-Baptist-to-the-bone woman like my mama, the Sabbath definitely meant Sunday, not the twenty-four-hour time period from sundown on Friday night through sundown on Saturday night observed by those who follow a more Judaic or literal Old Testament tradition. In my mama's world, "holy" meant not only did I have to use my inside voice while clad in a prissy dress and uncomfortable shoes for the better part of the day we spent at church, it also meant I couldn't swim in a two-piece bathing suit when we got home. Nor was Dad allowed to mow the lawn that day, lest the neighbors notice our family "working" on a Sunday! Thankfully, our pool was in the backyard surrounded by a privacy fence, so at least she allowed us to swim on hot Sunday afternoons. But my sister and I had to wear one-piece bathing suits—I guess belly buttons are bad news on the Lord's Day. (I repeated that phrase as a child with hushed reverence and apprehension since I'd rebelled a few times and sneakily wore my verboten bikini on the Sunday afternoons my mom left home to visit relatives. I half-expected to be zapped by divine lightning at any given moment.)

Fortunately, for those of us who've mistakenly associated the Sabbath with strictly enforced rules about external stuff like neck-to-knee splashing attire and the appropriate days of the week to engage in lawn care, we're about to find out how the passages God gave us regarding the Sabbath are much more about love than legalism.

> Since stretching always involves movement, please stand up and read the following two Sabbath passages out loud slowly: Exodus 20:8-11 and Leviticus 23:1-3. (If you're not able to walk, please do whatever you can to shift your posture, even if it's only a slight adjustment.) Then read them through a second time with a different tone and cadence. What words did you emphasize in both passages? Why did they strike you as more important than the other words?

1. Rest
2.

How would you synopsize the seven verses you just read into one single statement?

*take a break from the busy-ness of your life to ponder the glory of God and all he has done*

If you were explaining these passages to a child, how would you describe them and apply them?

Based on my dear, well-intentioned mom's understanding of what Christians couldn't do on Sundays—no bearing of belly buttons, no loud talking, no loud music, no lawn mowing, no playing freeze tag, no bike riding, no TV watching, no loitering at Burger King with friends—by the time I could read, I had deduced that God was a grumpy disciplinarian, determined to make His kids well-behaved rule followers, even if it meant quashing their joy once a week.

Therefore, it's been such a sweet relief to discover that God established these rest and renewal parameters for our benefit and not to censor six-year-olds in bikinis! Jesus emphasized this point when He proclaimed, "The Sabbath was made for man and not man for the Sabbath" (Mark 2:27), after some uppity killjoys masquerading as spiritual leaders made a fuss about His disciples harvesting a little grain on the Lord's Day because they were hungry. Over and over again (as illustrated in the passages below), our Redeemer pushed back against those who tried to twist God's Word into a tool through which they could condemn, shame, or subjugate others.

Read Mark 3:1-6; Luke 13:10-17; 14:1-6; John 5:1-18; 9:1-41. What common language do you notice in these New Testament healing-on-the-Sabbath stories?

*The love Jesus has for people who are afflicted. Also the hard-hearts of the Pharisees who only want to find something to blame Jesus*

Jesus demonstrated a proverbial new "dance move" when He stepped on the toes of Pharisees who were offended by the aforementioned healings in light of their advocation for a strict, literal enforcement of the Sabbath law. What would you describe as the overarching theme of that dance move?

*Compassion*

In each of these stories, we hear and sense the indignant attitudes of the religious leaders. Their quest for pious living had caused them to lose focus of the meaning of the Sabbath. They were more concerned with keeping tradition than showing mercy and grace.[3] Living by the letter of the Law blinded them to the needs of the people. They were keeping the people bound while Jesus was setting them free.

Read 2 Corinthians 3:4-6. In this passage, the apostle Paul makes a distinction between the "letter" of the old covenant, which kills, and the "Spirit" of the new covenant (or the gospel), which gives life (v. 6). In light of his delineation, what do you think would be the most life-giving results for you of observing a Sabbath/rest day every week?

# Learning Redemptive Rhythms

One of the first rules I established when Missy's adoption was finalized and I finally got to bring her home was that she had to hold my hand when we were walking anywhere cars could be present. That rule applied to parking lots, city sidewalks, or even along some peaceful path in a suburban neighborhood. I was a stickler about enforcing that policy too. Missy grew up in a very rural Haitian village, so she had limited experience with traffic or the fatal damage automobiles can do when they come into contact with flesh and bone. But since my child is a wonderfully feisty and independent leader, she sometimes balked at the holding-mom's-hand guideline, wanting to run ahead of me. So I called a family meeting between the two of us and employed the use of the word *pancake*. It's one of the few English words Missy understood at the time and a term that had quickly become dear to her because, much like her adoptive mama, my kid's a big fan of carbs!

Once I had her complete attention by getting the pancake mix out of the pantry, stirring the necessary ingredients together and pouring the first soon-to-be-edible circle on a hot griddle, I said, "Missy, do you want a pancake?" She nodded enthusiastically and exclaimed, "Oui, manman blan!" ("Yes, white mama" in Creole).

While she was happily munching her second favorite breakfast food (sausage biscuits are the love of her life and remain firmly in the coveted number one position), I explained that the reason I make her hold my hand in the parking lot at Target, on the way to school, and when we're shopping in downtown Franklin is because she's little, so drivers have a harder time seeing her than they do a bigger, taller person like me.

Then, much to her surprise, I took another pancake off the griddle and plopped it directly on the table in front of her plate. Then I soberly said, "Honey, if a driver doesn't see you and runs you over with his car or truck, you'll be squashed flat just like this pancake." My sweet baby girl looked stunned for a moment, then sadly mumbled through a mouthful of food, "I don't wanna be a pancake, Mama."

I didn't make up some dogma about hand-holding around cars to squeeze all the gleeful running-ahead-of-mama fun out of my daughter's day. I did so because I love her and wanted to protect her life.

How much more does our heavenly Father love His kids? Could it be that He sets biblical parameters in place for our good?

> If your answer to the above question is yes, what redemptive fences have you run into recently?

> Read Acts 15:10-11,28-29. Does the point Peter and the early church leaders made about God not wanting these new Gentile believers to have to "be saddled with any crushing burden" (v. 28, MSG) fit with your current understanding of God's character and His requirements? Or is this description more tender than your previous image of who God is? Explain.

I often forget to read the Old Testament laws in light of the socio-historical context in which they were given. Let me tell you, that'll flat put a clog in your understanding-God's-grace plumbing! We have to remember that when our heavenly Father initially enforced the guidelines regarding the Sabbath in Exodus 16:27-30, the Israelites—the people group God chose to establish as a theocracy and set His favor on to illustrate His covenantal love for humanity—had just followed Moses out of Egypt after four hundred years in captivity. They were as wobbly as newborn calves when it came to this whole liberation thing, having no experience or understanding of what freedom felt like. For as long as their grandparents and great-grandparents and great-great-grandparents could remember, they'd existed as slaves under the mostly cruel ownership of the Egyptians. A Jewish slave's sole purpose in Egyptian culture during that era was to do the brutal, backbreaking work—like mixing mud and straw to make bricks and hauling heavy stones in the oppressive Middle Eastern heat—their overseers didn't want to do. And there was no such thing as vacation days or sick leave. A slave's workday began early and ended late every single day.

There was no clear light at the end of the tunnel for an Israelite slave during the Egyptian captivity. Their only practical hope was for a master who wasn't overly abusive.

But God!

He texted Moses through a flaming topiary and set in motion an audacious plan to rescue His people. The plan included plagues that would surely traumatize even the most experienced pest control person and added a supernatural exclamation point of the sea doing splits! I can only imagine how shell-shocked those Hebrews were by the time they set up camp at the base of Mount Sinai shortly after watching the Egyptian army—who was in hot pursuit of them—get swallowed up by the Red Sea. Their entire lives had been spent in captivity and now, suddenly, their chains were gone, manna was raining down like donuts from heaven, and Yaweh was hovering over them like a protective parent.

Perhaps they had been enslaved for so long that they completely forgot what freedom felt like.

Now meditate on these words again in the Living Bible paraphrase:

> Remember to observe the Sabbath as a holy day. Six days a week are for your daily duties and your regular work, but the seventh day is a day of Sabbath rest before the Lord your God. On that day you are to do no work of any kind, nor shall your son, daughter, or slaves—whether men or women—or your cattle or your house guests. For in six days the Lord made the heaven, earth, and sea, and everything in them, and rested the seventh day; so he blessed the Sabbath day and set it aside for rest.

**EXODUS 20:8-11, TLB**

Sounds more like a much-needed reprieve than a punitive rule, doesn't it? As does the reiteration of God's protective parameters in Leviticus:

> GOD spoke to Moses: "Tell the People of Israel, These are my appointed feasts, the appointed feasts of GOD which you are to decree as sacred assemblies. Work six days. The seventh day is a Sabbath, a day of total and complete rest, a sacred assembly. Don't do any work. Wherever you live, it is a Sabbath to GOD.

**LEVITICUS 23:1-3, MSG**

It was like God was saying: "You matter so much to Me that I'm not willing to allow you to work your fingers to the bone any longer! Therefore, I've established a twenty-four-hour, no-labor time period so that you can relax and be refueled by leaning into My presence. I want you to sleep late and have the luxury of sitting at the dining table with your family and lingering over a great meal and laughing at your children's jokes. You are My beloved, and every single moment of your life exists under the canopy of My grace. But you need to take regular breaks from your busyness to focus on Me and My gifts for you in order to remember that."

The Bible was never intended to be used as a club. If we make the mistake of reading it as a rule book, we'll whack the joy and peace out of ourselves and others pretty quickly. If we don't take the time to marinate in the context and life-giving intent behind the words God spoke, we may inaccurately apply it with soul-sucking consequences. But when we do take the time to meditate on how incredibly redemptive God has been throughout human history, even the seemingly anti-belly button parts of it can begin to bring us joy and contentment!

Has there been any inherited theology you've felt the need to unlearn as an adult? If so, what did you strive to unlearn? Why?

Read Matthew 12:1-8. When Jesus was asked a question about the Sabbath, why do you think He deferred to a narrative—a story—from Torah rather than to the legal sections of Torah?

Jesus wasn't trying to debate them about the veracity of the Law. He wasn't challenging the Law itself, just their interpretation of it. The religious leaders had made the Law confining in a you-can't-wear-your-bikini-or-cut-the-grass kind of way. Jesus brought in the compassion element. This wasn't about restrictions but freedom.

Read 2 Chronicles 30:17-22. God granted the priests a significant degree of freedom in allowing people who weren't ceremonially clean to worship. Hezekiah had interceded for the people, asking God to pardon those whose hearts were seeking Him even if they hadn't followed the letter of the Law. What degree of freedom do you feel God has given you with regard to how and when you carve out time for rest and renewal (i.e., a practical Sabbath)?

# Following God's Lead

The fresh truth God revealed when I took the time to really meditate on what the Bible says about Sabbath is this—when God crashed out on a celestial couch in Genesis 2:1-3 after creating the universe, it was *before* sin entered the garden through a slithery, lying fruit salesman. Remember, Eve took the rebellious bite in Genesis 3, which means Sabbath wasn't only a necessary accomodation for our pitiable human weakness. Instead, God created and modeled rest as part of His perfect plan for His image bearers. It's an awesome and unblemished gift, not a consolation prize!

> On the scale of one to ten below regarding busyness—with 1 being a couch potato and 10 being racing around like a chicken with your head cut off—circle the number that best represents how you're feeling today.

1    (2)    3    4    5    6    7    8    9    10

> Does resting in God's presence come naturally to you, or do you have to work at it?

*I have to work at it a bit, but usually I look forward to spending time in God's presence*

> Read Matthew 11:28-30? What is the heaviest burden you're carrying in this season? What do you think needs to happen for that burden to become lighter? Are you willing to exchange your burden for Jesus' "yoke" (v. 29), which is a harness type of device used for placing an animal in service and therefore implies submitting yourself to His plans and purposes? Why or why not?

*My heart is willing, but in my head I keep thinking about what I can do to fix this burden.*

I'm a natural extrovert and a Three on the Enneagram, which means I'm pretty driven by productivity and accomplishment. It also means that when I'm not attuned with God's Spirit, I tend to associate my worth with my work. And unfortunately, the biblically indefensible lies that sometimes still rattle around

in my hard head—*You are what you do; You're only as good as your last win*— are ingrained in the modern psyche as a whole. All one has to do is flip on the television for a few hours of numbing distraction or scroll through social media while waiting for a barista to finish frothing a $5 coffee to find more than enough substantive proof that our culture is preoccupied with performance and productivity. Probably because *doing* can be observed from a distance—you don't have to get your hands dirty or heart involved. Doing can be tweeted and FaceTimed and livestreamed. It can be critiqued and panned and bullied. But *being* is much quieter, less noticable, and difficult to replicate or judge.

So what does that mean for followers of Christ who are seeking to have more meaningful, Jesus-shaped lives? Well, I think it means we need to converse with God before scrolling through comments on social media. It means listening to God's voice before using ours. It means becoming so deeply encouraged by our Redeemer's affirmation through His Word and prayer that we're rendered largely deaf to human applause. It means we live in the light of His love so that our desperate need for validation from others shrivels up and dies like an unwatered houseplant. It means we follow God's consistently redemptive lead instead of the changing whims and addictions of a broken world. It means that, much like those who traipsed after Moses in the wilderness, we finally have the chance to be free and experience the rhythms of purposeful work and regular intervals of rest that our Father lovingly established in order for us to live our best lives.

If that sounds good to you, I invite you to find a relatively quiet place where you can be alone for at least ten minutes. Then, reopen your Bible to Exodus 20:8-11, and slowly read through the passage again, pausing to converse with God about each phrase or word you find interesting. Talk to Him about what stands out to you and how your heart is responding. Ask Him for clarification and wisdom. Talk to Him about when and how your mind is wandering, and ask Him to reveal what's behind your restlessness. If you're comfortable doing so, feel free to use the lines below to journal your prayers and how you sense the Holy Spirit guiding you with regard to rest.

---------------------------------------------------------------

---------------------------------------------------------------

---------------------------------------------------------------

---------------------------------------------------------------

Reread Leviticus 23:1-3, and write a responsive prayer that corresponds to statements and phrases in the passage. Here's a template you can follow:

**GOD'S HEART:** The LORD spoke to Moses: "Speak to the Israelites and tell them ..." (vv. 1-2a).

**MY HEART:** Thank you for choosing to speak to us, God!

*Thank you God for speaking to my heart. You remind me that you are in control of all circumstances because sometimes I think I can change things myself!*

**GOD'S HEART:** "These are my appointed times, the times of the LORD that you will proclaim as sacred assemblies" (v. 2b).

**MY HEART:** Lord, please teach me to plan my calendar around Your purposes instead of my preferences.

**GOD'S HEART:** "Work may be done for six days, but on the seventh day there is to be a Sabbath of complete rest, a sacred assembly" (v. 3a).

**MY HEART:** Thank You for loving me enough to make my rest and restoration a sacred priority, Jesus.

--------------------------------------------------------------------------------

--------------------------------------------------------------------------------

--------------------------------------------------------------------------------

--------------------------------------------------------------------------------

--------------------------------------------------------------------------------

--------------------------------------------------------------------------------

**GOD'S HEART:** "You are not to do any work; it is a Sabbath to the LORD wherever you live" (v. 3b).

**MY HEART:** Wherever I live and whatever I do, I want Your Spirit to steward my attention and affection, Father.

--------------------------------------------------------------------------------

--------------------------------------------------------------------------------

--------------------------------------------------------------------------------

--------------------------------------------------------------------------------

--------------------------------------------------------------------------------

--------------------------------------------------------------------------------

# Dancing For Good

I had an encounter not too long ago that has me contemplating salsa lessons (the dance, not the dip). I was teaching at a retreat for a large church where wiggling during the praise and worship time wasn't even remotely encouraged. (The constrained atmosphere there was not unlike that of the fictional town in *Footloose!*) Yet for some reason—let's hope it was the prompting of the Holy Spirit—I felt compelled to expound on the final two hallelujah psalms, Psalms 149 and 150. (The last five psalms in the Psalter are often referred to as "the hallelujah psalms," and many Old Testament scholars teach that they correspond to the five thematic books within the Book of Psalms itself.) These two psalms contain clear directives exhorting God's people to dance with abandon while praising Him (Ps. 149:3; 150:4).

Suffice it to say, my message was received with a lot of crossed arms and very few amens.

But afterward, a soft-spoken woman approached me and said she was pleasantly surprised that I brought up the topic of dancing in Scripture. She went on to explain how a few days before the retreat, she sensed God whispering, *I want you to learn to dance with Me*, during a time of prayer. She continued sheepishly, "Because I'm black, people tend to assume I have good rhythm, but I've actually never been much of a dancer. I've always been more serious-minded than free-spirited. So when God asked me to dance, I initially felt very self-conscious and awkward." Then she smiled broadly before confessing, "But when you started talking about dancing this morning in this environment, I clearly heard God whisper again. And this time He told me to stop watching my feet and just look at His face."

As we wrap up this first session of *How Much More*, let's endeavor to remember that the biblical context of resting—that spiritual dance in which we're learning to gaze at God instead of worrying about our footwork—isn't a punitive decree; it's God's generous endowment for our protection and perseverance. Practically speaking, the rest and renewal we can experience through Sabbath will help us become better ambassadors of the gospel message. Because if we're always uptight and overcommitted, I don't think the world is going to observe our stressed-out vibe and believe us when we proclaim that Jesus gives a peace that passes all understanding, right?

God gives us time to rest for our own good and for His kingdom purposes!

Frankly, it's important to reflect on how the redemptive parameters of Scripture affect us personally and help usher in God's will for the world around us. Because no matter how many verses we've highlighted in our Bibles, if we aren't actively loving our neighbors, then we're kidding ourselves about being Christlike. The bottom line is, our theology must inform our sociology. So let's start by intentionally carving out ongoing respites through which we can practice what we plan to preach!

Read Psalm 23 and Mark 6:30-32 before rereading Exodus 20:8-11 and Leviticus 23:1-3. What common thematic denominator(s) do you notice in these four passages?

Has Jesus made you "lie down" (Ps. 23:2) during a season when it wasn't your natural inclination to be still? Looking back on that divinely-forced rest, would you classify it as mean-spirited or merciful? Explain.

Describe your current "green pastures" or "quiet waters" (Ps. 23:2), the place you go to be alone with God and rest. What, if anything, could you do to make that space more inviting and conducive to meeting with your Creator Redeemer?

Because the fall season is right around the corner here in Tennessee, and the weather's beginning to turn cooler, Missy and I have had the pleasure of relaxing outside by the firepit in the evenings. Oftentimes, long moments will pass without any conversation between us while we simply enjoy watching our dogs play in the field below or admire the light show of late-season fireflies sending luminescent love notes to each other underneath the canopy of cedar trees in our backyard. It was during one of those recent quiet moments of contentment that Missy, who's now eleven years old, got up from where she was sitting and came over and crawled into my lap like she used to when she was little. It took a lot more shifting and repositioning because her arms and legs are almost as long as mine, but once she finally got settled comfortably against my chest, she sighed happily and said softly, "I know I'm not a baby anymore, Mom, but I sure do love sitting like this with you."

I think that's how God designed His kids too. When we lean back fully and completely relax in His arms, that's where we find our happy place … our sweet spot. That is Sabbath.

# Wonderful, Weighty Words

The following theological terms can help you better comprehend and communicate the *how much more* aspect of God's love, or, at the very least, help you impress folks at future dinner parties!

**A FORTIORI:** (derived from Latin) "An argument meaning 'with greater force' used in logic. It's found in traditional Jewish rules of interpretation to indicate what one can infer from a biblical text.[4] It's often used in conjunction with the Latin phrase *a minore ad majus*—'from the lesser to the greater'—which is a principle of biblical interpretation going back to Rabbi Hillel's major rules of interpretation where it means 'from the easy to the difficult.'"[5] The *how much more* idea is found in Matthew 7:11: "If you then, who are evil, know how to give good gifts to your children, how much more will your Father in heaven give good things to those who ask him." (See also Luke 11:13; Rom. 11:12; and Heb. 9:13-14.)

**IMAGO DEI:** "The Latin term for 'image of God' typically used in reference to Genesis 1:26-27 when God declares: Let us make man in our image, according to our likeness…so God created man in his own image; he created him in the image of God; he created them male and female. In God's work of creation, the crowning act, the pinnacle of that divine work, was the creation of human beings. It was to humans that God assigned and stamped His divine image. That we are created in the image of God gives to us the highest place among earthly beings. That image provides human beings with a unique ability to mirror and reflect the very character of God."[6]

**PRAXIS:** "A term taken directly from the Greek, literally meaning 'deed, action, or activity.' The basis for its contemporary use lies in two ideas: first, theoretical reflection arises out of active commitment, and therefore the criterion for right thinking (orthodoxy) is right action (orthopraxis); second, in turn, the goal of right thinking is the transformation of the world. Praxis denotes the kind of active commitment that leads to theoretical reflection. The use of praxis in this sense seeks to bring about the uniting of, or the overcoming of, such conceptual dualities as theory and practice, belief and action, or commitment and its ethical outworking."[7] For example, giving a gift for the sole reason of getting something back in return isn't actually giving a gift, because by definition a gift is free.

# Extra Credit Sabbath Information for Inquiring Minds:

"The Heb noun šabbāt, 'sabbath,' occurs 111 times in the OT. Concentrations of usage are in the Pentateuch with 47 times (Exodus 15 times; Leviticus 25 times; Numbers 4 times; Deuteronomy 3 times), the prophetic literature with 32 times (Ezekiel 15 times; Isaiah 8 times; Jeremiah 7 times; Amos and Hosea 1 time each), and the historical books with 30 times (Nehemiah 14 times; 1–2 Chronicles 10 times; 2 Kings 6 times). It appears one time each in Ps 92:1 and Lam 2:6. The noun šabbātôn, 'sabbath feast,' seems to be a derivative of the noun šabbāt (GKC §240) and appears eleven times. It is used by itself in Exod 16:23; 31:15; Lev 23:24, 39 in the sense of "sabbath feast" and in Lev 25:6 for 'the sabbath of the land,' i.e., the sabbatical year. The combination šabbāt šabbātôn, 'sabbath of complete/solemn rest,' appears for the seventh day (Exod 32:5; Lev 23:3), the annual Day of Atonement (Lev 16:31; 23:32), the annual Feast of Trumpets (Lev 23:24) and the sabbatical year (Lev 25:4). ...The NT has 67 usages of the term sábbaton (Synoptics 43 times; John 13 times; the remaining usages appear in Acts and in a few letters). In some usages the plural form (Matt 28:1; Mark 16:2; Luke 24:1; John 20:1, 19; Acts 20:27) or the singular (Luke 18:12; Mark 16:9; 1 Cor 16:2) refers to 'week'; otherwise the meaning is always the seventh day of the week, the sabbath."[8]

# How Much More

## LIBERATING IS THE WILL OF GOD THAN THE WAYS OF MAN

When you buy a Hebrew slave, he is to serve
for six years; then in the seventh he is to leave
as a free man without paying anything. ...

When a man strikes his male or female slave with a rod, and
the slave dies under his abuse, the owner must be punished.
However, if the slave can stand up after a day or two, the owner
should not be punished because he is his owner's property. ...

When an ox gores a man or a woman to death, the ox must be
stoned, and its meat may not be eaten, but the ox's owner is
innocent. However, if the ox was in the habit of goring, and
its owner has been warned yet does not restrain it, and it
kills a man or a woman, the ox must be stoned, and its owner
must also be put to death. If instead a ransom is demanded
of him, he can pay a redemption price for his life in the full
amount demanded from him. If it gores a son or a daughter,
he is to be dealt with according to this same law. If the ox
gores a male or female slave, he must give thirty shekels of
silver to the slave's master, and the ox must be stoned.

**EXODUS 21:2,20-21,28-32**

## Session Two: INHERITING GRACE FROM MR. Z'S GIRLS

To access the video teaching sessions, use the
instructions in the back of your Bible study book.

## DISCUSSION QUESTIONS

What impacted you the most from the video teaching?

How have you seen God show His love, care, and redemption in a difficult or tragic circumstance in your life or in the life of someone close to you?

Why do you think God's character gets such a bad rap in the Old Testament? Did you ever have a negative view of the God you saw in the Old Testament? Explain.

Have you ever been guilty of fashioning God in your own image? What is the consequence of doing that?

Lisa said we're not bold enough because we don't believe enough. What does that mean? Do you agree? Explain.

Do you absolutely believe that God is for you? If not, why not? If so, how does your faith walk and prayer life give evidence of your belief?

How did this video teaching reveal the redemptive heart and extravagant love of God?

# Stretching Sacred Muscles

"Michael Jordan, perennial basketball champion" probably isn't the first thought that would come to your mind if you met my mom. First of all, she's petite—maybe five feet, three inches if she's wearing heels. Secondly, she's a bit of a Southern belle, so her superior athleticism is usually well camouflaged by a lovely blouse and pearls. Plus, she's eighty-three, so the idea of her crashing the boards for a rebound does seem a tad absurd.

But let me tell you, my mama was indeed a baller. In fact, she was so good at basketball that my stepfather, Dad Angel, built a partial court in our backyard, complete with regulation rim and markings for the free throw/foul shot key.

When I was growing up, Mom shot hoops pretty much every day (except Sundays, of course!). Her normal routine was to start at the top of the key and then run through fifty layups from the right side, followed by fifty layups on the left side. She finished up with fifty free throws. And her accuracy was uncanny; she hardly ever missed.

That's why when our high school athletic department announced they were having a fundraiser, wherein faculty members (mostly the coaching staff) would get sponsors to donate money according to how many free throws they made in a certain amount of time, my friends and I cajoled Mom into signing up.

I'll never forget the look on the faces of the male coaches when Patti Angel—the not-a-hair-out-of-place assistant school librarian—strode elegantly into the gym and asked where she could sign up. I think they assumed it was a prank. Their assumption was quickly disproved the day of the fundraiser when Mom sank one hundred free throws in a row in less than five minutes, thereby winning the entire contest and earning the stunned admiration of the entire high school athletic department in the process!

My friends and I thoroughly embarrassed her in the days and weeks that followed by whooping it up and recounting her performance over and over again. Mom's amazing feat of free throw wizardry became the stuff of local legend. For years afterward, if she encountered one of the coaches when she was running errands around town, they'd either wax nostalgic about her accomplishment or perform a "we're not worthy" bow with teasing—albeit affectionate—exaggeration.

Not long after her roundball prowess was made public, Mom quietly confessed to me that her determination to succeed at basketball had been fueled by the stinging assessment from several adults in her childhood who viewed her left-handedness as a physical limitation. A few had even predicted that "Patti Ann" would be a complete failure when it came to any athletic pursuit. One of my mom's Sunday School teachers went so far as to use the following Bible passages to "prove" left-handedness was a liability:

> Joseph said to his father, "Not that way, my father! This one is the firstborn. Put *your right hand* on his head."

### GENESIS 48:18, EMPHASIS MINE

> LORD, *your right hand* is glorious in power.
> LORD, *your right hand* shattered the enemy. ...
> You stretched out *your right hand*,
> and the earth swallowed them.

### EXODUS 15:6,12, EMPHASIS MINE

Like me, you probably rolled your eyes inwardly over the small-mindedness of some yahoo twisting Scripture to shame a little girl over her dominant hand. If Mom's old Sunday School teacher had simply taken the time to thumb through a basic concordance, she would've found a Bible reference that actually lauds left-handedness—Judges 3:12-30. In that passage, God intentionally used left-handed Ehud to slay an evil king who was opposed to the Israelites.

From a twenty-first century vantage point, it's easy to recognize that the concept of left-handed inferiority was culturally relative and has proven to be bogus. I mean, even if you don't dig up biblical evidence, all you have to do is google the salaries of southpaw pitchers in major league baseball to ascertain that being a left-handed athlete is anything but a liability now!

However, there are lots of other practices in Scripture that aren't nearly as simple to categorize as "culturally bound." And unfortunately, many ethics—like sexual purity and personal holiness—that God never intended to be discarded, are being jettisoned and wrongly labeled as no longer relevant in modernity. So we're going to keep stretching our hearts and minds to better understand some of the stickier issues in the Bible, whether or not God intended them to develop

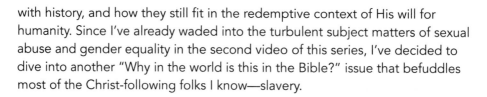

with history, and how they still fit in the redemptive context of His will for humanity. Since I've already waded into the turbulent subject matters of sexual abuse and gender equality in the second video of this series, I've decided to dive into another "Why in the world is this in the Bible?" issue that befuddles most of the Christ-following folks I know—slavery.

In light of the recent global protests, violence, and public division we've experienced with regard to power structures built—at least partly—on ethnic discrimination, the subjugation of one people group for the benefit of another people group in biblical narrative is an extremely pertinent, and perhaps even volatile, issue that all but begs redemptive clarification. The fact that many white confessing Christians, including pastors, in the past actually used the Bible to establish chattel slavery as a norm—even a "God-ordained right" by some—is a wound that must be lanced. It's very important to note that slavery mentioned in the Bible was usually different than the type of slavery practiced in the colonial-era United States. In ancient history people sometimes chose to sell themselves into slavery for a season to pay off debt. But they weren't considered the sole property/chattel of someone else, nor was the type of slavery recorded in Scripture always based on ethnicity. American slavery cannot be shoved under the rug of "it didn't happen on our watch" by today's Christ followers. Not if we want to have a credible, compassionate voice in modern culture or, perhaps even more importantly, with precious family members, friends, neighbors, and coworkers who've been bloodied and bruised by people who claim to love God but actively oppose, vilify, and subjugate other image bearers based on perceived biological and theological "evidence," which is actually hateful heresy.

> Read the Book of Philemon. How good of God to give us this true story of how Paul advocated for Onesimus's freedom to keep us mindful that His will is never for anyone to be enslaved. What might it look like for you to put Paul's compassionate plea in verse 17 into practice with regard to others in your community who've been marginalized and mistreated because of racial-ethnic discrimination?

Read Psalm 111:10; Jeremiah 10:12; Romans 11:33; and
1 Corinthians 1:18-25. How would you encapsulate those
verses into one statement about God?

Read Psalm 103:14 and Romans 7:15-20, and review
1 Corinthians 1:18-20. Contrary to God's character, the
Bible makes it clear that humans are neither omniscient nor
perfectly wise. How might our lack of brilliance factor into God
shepherding us slowly toward what's for our good and His glory?

What ungodly habits and sinful behaviors (i.e., gossip, jealousy,
gluttony, impatience, cheating on your taxes, watching soft porn
that masquerades as a sitcom, and so forth) are you still trying to
overcome?

# Learning Redemptive Rhythms

One of the most heart-wrenching habits I had to help Missy break during the first few months after she came home from Haiti was flinching. When I raised my hand to fix her bow or straighten her collar or carress her cheek, she'd recoil every time. It was obvious that Missy had received enough blows in her past to create deep-seated fear that surfaced whenever my hand got too close to her head or face. She soon learned enough English to express what she was feeling when she ducked. She'd point to her face and tell me about a lady at the orphanage who hit her. The first time she said it, I picked her up and held her for a long time, explaining softly over and over again that I would never, ever slap her in the face, hit her on the head, or intentionally hurt her. Once she finally relaxed and fell asleep in my arms, I laid her on the bed, pulled the covers up around her, walked out of her room, leaned against the wall, and wept.

I'll never forget the look of terror that washed over Missy's face when she thought I was going to strike her. Or the angst of realizing that sometimes she was afraid of me. I still grieve the reality that my baby girl ever had to endure any type of abuse. But at the beginning of our mother-daughter relationship, I also grieved that Missy didn't yet know the real me. I can't help thinking that all too often God's children tend to see Him in a similar fashion—we don't trust that He's good, that He's for us and never against us. Unfortunately, the words of Scripture He breathed to bless us have sometimes been eggregiously carved out of context to curse us, which is most certainly the case with slavery.

Quite frankly, it's easy to understand how people can misconstrue biblical texts when taken out of their socio-historical context. But anytime someone uses Scripture to malign, mistreat, or murder, you can bet it's being twisted to justify something our Creator Redeemer never intended. Just because something that was part of history is recorded in the Bible doesn't mean God approves of it.

Scripture is both descriptive and prescriptive. It's like a yearbook that records human history and literary medicine that establishes a way to redeem human history. Therefore, while the Bible chronicles the messiest chapters of humankind since Adam's first breath, it doesn't condone the sinful carnage we've perpetrated since he and Eve stumbled out of the garden of Eden. Instead, Scripture sets a new course through which we can repent, submit to God's plan, and find our way back to the perfect peace, hope, and joy He intended for us through a relationship with Him. The bottom line is that our heavenly Father didn't create slavery any more than He created evil practices like child sacrifice, rape, or murder. Humankind did. However, God has been actively and consistently restraining the cruel and oppressive practice of slavery since its inception.

For instance, just a few books to the right of Exodus—and a few steps further on the continuum of human history—you'll find the parameters regarding owning another human being beginning to shift significantly.

> If your fellow Hebrew, a man or woman, is sold to you and
> serves you six years, you must set him free in the seventh year.
> When you set him free, do not send him away empty-handed.
> Give generously to him from your flock, your threshing floor,
> and your winepress. You are to give him whatever the LORD your
> God has blessed you with. Remember that you were a slave in
> the land of Egypt and the LORD your God redeemed you; that
> is why I am giving you this command today. But if your slave
> says to you, "I don't want to leave you," because he loves you
> and your family, and is well off with you, take an awl and pierce
> through his ear into the door, and he will become your slave for
> life. Also treat your female slave the same way. Do not regard
> it as a hardship when you set him free, because he worked
> for you six years—worth twice the wages of a hired worker.
> Then the LORD your God will bless you in everything you do.

### DEUTERONOMY 15:12-18

> Do not return a slave to his master when he has escaped
> from his master to you. Let him live among you wherever
> he wants within your city gates. Do not mistreat him.

### DEUTERONOMY 23:15-16

> If a man is discovered kidnapping one of his Israelite
> brothers, whether he treats him as a slave or sells him, the
> kidnapper must die. You must purge the evil from you.

### DEUTERONOMY 24:7

The first passage establishes generous provisions for a slave upon his release; the second establishes safety for runaway slaves; and the third denounces slave traders. It's important to note that these loosening of restrictions only occurred inside the Israelite culture during this ancient era of history. In the rest of the world, slaves were considered commodities to be bought, sold, bound, traded, abused, and killed with minimal negative consequences for the owner/abuser. But immediately after God's people were liberated from slavery (Deuteronomy was written shortly after Moses led the Israelites out of Egypt, where they'd been in bondage for centuries), He began teaching them more redemptive ways to regulate labor. He set up increasingly compassionate parameters through which they would learn to treat others with dignity, which was the opposite of the mistreatment they'd endured for generations. Those ancient image bearers were mere babes in the context of liberty, yet God was already showing them how to loosen the ties that bound other captives. This reveals our Creator's redemptive nature, even in the darkest nights of human history. It rekindles hope for humanity's future, as historian and theological scholar Jemar Tisby affirms in his recent book, *The Color of Compromise*:

> But if racism can be made, it can be unmade. Like a house with a crumbling foundation, it is more difficult to change an existing structure than to build a sound one from the beginning, but it is possible. "The fierce urgency of now," to borrow a phrase from Martin Luther King Jr., demands a recognition of the ways Christians, from before the founding of the United States, built racial categories into religion. That knowledge must then be turned toward propagating a more authentically biblical message of human equality regardless of skin color.[1]

In other words, the *how much more* truism of God's unconditional love will echo louder and louder as racial/ethnic-based discrimination is exposed and eradicated.

**Read Matthew 23:23-28.**

This passage reveals our Savior chastising some Pharisees for hypocritical behavior. Technically they were obeying the Law, but their hearts were anything but righteous. They were preoccupied with looking spiritual but missed the main point that true obedience is motivated by love for God, not legalism. Plus, living in light of God's promises and parameters will motivate us to love others, not lord religious superiority over them like the Pharisees were doing.

Can you think of an example from your own life (or maybe your child's life, if you're a parent) when the right thing was done but with the wrong heart attitude?

Read Psalm 119:1-8,159-60; John 14:15; and Revelation 22:18-19. How can we reconcile the **INERRANCY** of God's Word for His intended purposes with biblical themes that were obviously culturally bound and had no intertestamental continuity (which is just a fancy theological term I learned in seminary that basically means it didn't cross over from Old Testament culture to New Testament culture) like polygamy or not wearing linen and wool in the same garment? (See Deut. 22:11.)

Read Matthew 5:21-48.

When Jesus said, "You have heard," in this gospel passage He was referring to what had been previously taught regarding the Old Testament Law. But then He proclaimed, "But I tell you," and went on to give their original, Hebraic understanding of Scripture a bigger, more wholistic, and personally stretching application.

How does this "You have heard, but I tell you" template point to redemptive movement within the Bible?

Meditate for a few minutes on the passages you've read in this section and how they point to the redemptive character of God. Consider how you are reflecting that character in your own life.

# Following God's Lead

I don't for a moment want to present navigating complex issues like sexual abuse, misogyny, or slavery using God's Word as our ultimate guide as a simplistic, step-by-step process. I've been studying Scripture for more than thirty years as a vocational Bible teacher, earned a Master of Theological Studies from Covenant Seminary, am currently well beyond the halfway point in a doctoral program at Denver Seminary, and I'm still consistently wowed by wonderful truths I'm just now seeing in passages I'd perused hundreds of times before. I'm also repeatedly flummoxed by other passages I'd foolishly assumed I had totally figured out at some point in my walk of faith and now realize I misunderstood. The Bible is a supernatural, life-giving text, but it is not simple! Because the Old and New Testament Scriptures were first recorded in Hebrew, Greek, and Aramaic, there are nuances in the original grammar and syntax that aren't always perfectly transferable to the English language. It's also important for followers of Christ to recognize that every single syllable in both testaments had a first intended audience. Which means we need to be aware that there's a socio-historical context to what we cut and paste and splash across social media!

For instance, when Deuteronomy 22:8 was written—"When you build a new house, you shall make a parapet for your roof, that you may not bring the guilt of blood upon your house, if anyone should fall from it" (ESV)—Jews lived in homes with flat roofs. So if they had a rooftop shindig, there was a chance someone could get too close to the edge and fall off.[2] Therefore, a railing—a parapet—was a very good idea. Does that mean modern-day Christians are being disobedient heretics if they don't have railings around their rooflines? Nope. However, if you have a flat roof and plan to have parties up there, it's still the right thing to do to help ensure public safety. Plus, the existence of a parapet will definitely work in your favor in a personal injury lawsuit should some party guest become so stupefied after gobbling copious amounts of chips and queso (mind you, I'm just spitballing here) that he or she inadvertently stumbles over your gutter and tumbles into the bushes below!

The *principles* God gave His people—like establishing boundaries to ensure the physical safety of people in their homes—move forward regardless of culture. However, some of the *practices* chronicled in the Bible—like rooftop railings—are culturally relevant. When it comes to the painful subject of slavery, some of the practices—like not beating a slave to death—do not move forward because God never endorsed slavery in the first place. But the principles God began to teach the Israelites as He unfolded His plan to eradicate slavery—like valuing the lives and dignity of other people—are as pertinent and applicable today as they were then.

With that in mind, I invite you to find a relatively quiet place where you can be alone for at least ten minutes. Then open your Bible to Exodus 21 and slowly read through the verses at the beginning of this session (2,20-21,28-32). Then review Deuteronomy 15:12-18; 23:15-16; and 24:7. Finally, read 1 Corinthians 7:20-24; 12:13; and Galatians 3:28.

> Talk to God about what stands out to you as a *time-bound practice* and what stands out to you as a *timeless principle*. Ask Him for wisdom regarding what freedom should look like in our culture. Ask Him to reveal relationships or environments where you have consciously or subconsciously ignored, avoided, mistreated, or acted condescendingly toward people who are racially or ethnically different than you, then confess and repent as the Holy Spirit prompts you to do so.

Feel free to use the lines below to journal your prayers, noting how you sense the Holy Spirit guiding you with regard to modern-day slavery (human trafficking), racial discrimination, oppressive hierarchical structures, and personal liberties.

A timebound principal I see is that
you, God, wants people to be Kind and
loving to each other.
I pray you will guide Brittany to forgive
her sister and be filled with your love
and peace

Read Colossians 3:11-17 and Philemon 8-18, and write a responsive prayer that corresponds to the overarching theme/God's heart in both of these passages. (To help you get started, see the similar exercise in Session One on page 25.)

**GOD'S HEART:**

**MY HEART:**

_____

_____

_____

_____

_____

_____

_____

**GOD'S HEART:**

**MY HEART:**

_____

_____

_____

_____

_____

_____

_____

**GOD'S HEART:**

**MY HEART:**

---------------------------------------------------------------------------------

---------------------------------------------------------------------------------

---------------------------------------------------------------------------------

---------------------------------------------------------------------------------

---------------------------------------------------------------------------------

---------------------------------------------------------------------------------


**GOD'S HEART:**

**MY HEART:**

---------------------------------------------------------------------------------

---------------------------------------------------------------------------------

---------------------------------------------------------------------------------

---------------------------------------------------------------------------------

---------------------------------------------------------------------------------

---------------------------------------------------------------------------------

# Dancing For Good

Several years ago, I sold Missy's favorite motorcycle—a huge yellow Honda with an "Adoption Rocks" sidecar personalized just for her. A disturbing incident was my impetus for selling. One day while we were cruising down a country road, two young men in a truck flying a large rebel flag from their tailgate pulled up next to us and started hurling soda cans and shouting expletives coupled with the N-word at us. I stared straight ahead and slowed down, praying they'd pass us quickly, especially in light of how vulnerable we were on a motorcycle. Instead, they veered directly in front of us, forcing me to crash our motorcycle into the ditch. By the grace of God we weren't physically injured, but I knew my little girl's heart was deeply wounded. So as soon as we were able to get the bike out of the ditch and limp home, I sat Missy in front of me on the couch and said, "Baby, I want to talk to you about what just happened with those guys in the truck." She replied with sad bewilderment, "Why were they so mean to us, Mama?"

She was only six. I thought I'd have more time to explain the ugly and evil reality of racism. A lump formed in my throat as I took both of her tiny hands in mine and said, "Honey, some people have really little lives. They only hang around with other people who look like them and talk like them and think like them. And sometimes, when you choose to live a really little life, your heart and mind get smaller too because they don't have room to grow." I was then going to warn my beautiful Haitian daughter about how we need to be prepared and alert when we find ourselves in certain, potentially dangerous environments, but she interrupted me and exclaimed brightly, "I know what we need to do, Mama! We need to help their hearts get bigger!"

World and national events, along with what Missy overhears at school, have prompted me to have many more similar, increasingly candid conversations about prejudice, bigotry, and, of course, slavery in the years since the motorcycle incident. But Missy's philosophy hasn't wavered. She continually encourages me to help shriveled hearts get bigger. Somehow my kid sees what some adults, and even a contingency of the church, seem blind to—hating other image bearers is the antithesis of the gospel. Obviously, much more serious and hard work has to be done than just "helping people's hearts get bigger" to root out the horrific sin that upholds systemic racism and xenophobia. But I still think Missy is wise for her age to recognize that our hearts play a huge role in whether we choose to perpetrate hatred and injustice or choose to plow them up in order to pave the way for redemption like Paul did with Onesimus in his Letter to Philemon. And Proverbs seems to confirm my baby girl's intuition:

All a person's ways seem right to him, but the LORD weighs hearts.

**PROVERBS 21:2**

The good news is that we've had many other experiences that have diminished the rebel-flag-road-rage event as effectively as Dawn dish soap reduces grease. In fact, one took place only a few days afterward. Remembering how, when I was a little girl, my Dad Harper always encouraged me to get back on a horse that had bucked me off so that the fear of failure wouldn't win or have time to grow roots in my heart, I got Missy back on the bike. I didn't want racism to win in my daughter's psyche. Because I was probably more nervous than she was, I drove slower than usual, swiveling my head the whole time to make sure there were no trucks with rebel flags anywhere on the horizon. After we rode about ten miles from our house, I pulled over at a rural gas station/grocery store/deli called Huff's. I'd heard they had great sandwiches, and my plan was to pick up a couple, along with some of Missy's favorite chips and her beloved lemonade, then ride to a nearby park to enjoy an alfresco lunch.

But when we walked into that old, iconic country store (Huff's was built in 1911), I instinctively stiffened and put my hand protectively on Missy's shoulder. There were several men loitering around the counter who looked like they could be the daddies of those stinkers driving the truck that had edged us off the road. You probably know the type—big belt buckles, worn jeans, John Deere hats, scuffed boots, and one cheek bulging with tobacco. Basically, they looked just like my dear dad did before he strode into glory to meet Jesus. Unfortunately, in my experience, men who resemble my father don't always appreciate white mamas with beautiful black daughters. So with a growing sense of unease, I quickly gave our sandwich order to the man behind the counter, who I later learned was the store owner, Mr. Charlie Huff. He began cheerfully assembling our turkey, cheese, mayo, and fresh tomato concoctions thicker than I'd ever seen, all the while chatting it up with Missy:

Mr. Charlie: Hello darlin', my name's Charlie, what's yours?

Missy (somewhat shyly): My name's Missy Harper. I'm six.

Mr. Charlie: Well wouldn't you know it? My favorite age in the whole world is six! Which means I just have to put an extra slice of cheese on your sandwich to celebrate because you're the first six-year-old I've seen all day! Is that OK with you, honey? Do you like cheese?

Missy (shyness replaced by enthusiasm): YESSIR! I *love* cheese! My mom says I'm a cheese hound!

Mr. Charlie: Well, that does it then! I thought you and your mama looked familiar when you walked in. Y'all must be long-lost relatives! Which means you can call me "Uncle Charlie" now.

Missy (happily taking the bag of sandwiches from him while I slide my credit card to pay): Yes Sir, Mister, I mean Uncle Charlie! It sure was nice to meet you!

Mr. Charlie (chuckling): The pleasure's all mine, Miss Missy!

As we were walking out of the store, I turned back toward Charlie because I wanted to thank him for being so gracious and personable to my little girl. His genuine kindness was very different from the bigotry I expected to receive from the men who didn't exactly look like poster boys for diversity. Per usual, I got teary while I was trying to express my appreciation for his friendly inclusivity, because I almost always get choked up when I'm overwhelmed by unexpected grace. My emotive stammering startled Charlie and his cowboy-looking crew, and his features softened with empathy. It's as if he somehow already knew our tiny transracial family had been hurt by racism. He replied gently, "Oh Ma'am, we love all of God's children here at Huff's." Then he began introducing each one of those tough-on-the-outside, tender-on-the-inside gentlemen and explaining how several of them had grandchildren who were adopted from other cultures and backgrounds, just like Missy.

The tears spilling from my eyes barely allowed me to see through the plexiglass windshield of my helmet on the way to the park. The encounter with Uncle Charlie was a tangible reminder to never stop hoping for a better future than what we've experienced in the past. Our God is a Redeemer who always has been and always will be actively working on our behalf. Oh, and by the way, Missy and I ended up moving to a little "farmette" just a few miles down the road from Huff's a year after we met Charlie. Now he and Missy hang out on a

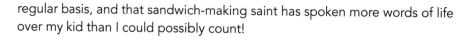

regular basis, and that sandwich-making saint has spoken more words of life over my kid than I could possibly count!

One of my favorite theologians, G. K. Chesterton, wrote this about Christians:

> We have come to the wrong star. ...That is what
> makes life at once so splendid and so strange. ...
> The true happiness is that we don't fit. We come
> from somewhere else. We have lost our way.[3]

In light of Sir Chesterton's brilliant yet poignant observation, I like to think of the Bible as a sort of supernatural telescope. Through it we can see up close the gross scars and imperfections that mar this spinning planet we call home— things like the evil enslavement of God's image bearers under the banner of economic profit, social propriety, or racial inferiority. But through the lens of Holy Writ we also get an increasingly clearer view of the glittering and flawless future that will be our divine inheritance. A glorious, pan-national place where saints from every tribe and tongue will worship God the Father, Jesus Christ the Son, and the Holy Spirit in a beautiful, multihued reflection of our Creator Redeemer:

> Then I saw a new heaven and a new earth; for the first heaven and
> the first earth had passed away, and the sea was no more.
> I also saw the holy city, the new Jerusalem, coming down out of
> heaven from God, prepared like a bride adorned for her husband.
> Then I heard a loud voice from the throne: Look, God's
> dwelling is with *humanity*, and he will live with them. They
> will be his *peoples*, and God himself will be with them and
> will be their God. He will wipe away every tear from their
> eyes. Death will be no more; grief, crying, and pain will be
> no more, because the previous things have passed away.

### REVELATION 21:1-4, EMPHASIS MINE

One of the best dancing for good moves we can make in light of the multicultural, bigotry-busting themes in Scripture is to respect and love well all of the other image bearers we have the privilege of rubbing shoulders with. And if, after taking an honest inventory of your community, you realize it's mostly homogenous, you probably need to be more intentional about developing real relationships with people outside of your comfort zone. A great place to start is to visit another Bible-based church where most of the worshipers come from different ethnic, racial, and/or sociodemographic backgrounds than you.

> Read Genesis 1:26-27; Colossians 3:9-11; and Revelation 7:9-10. Since God made humankind in His image and didn't choose to maintain one race or ethnicity—even early on in human history—and in light of the multicultural vision John had of heaven, what sound, biblical conclusions can we draw about racial or ethnic discrimination?

The Bible contains many of what scholars refer to as "vice and virtue" lists, representing core values that are widely regarded as transcultural because of their consistent appearance in both the Old and New Testaments.

> Read a few of the following passages for more clarity on what constitutes a biblical principle that doesn't "evolve" with history: Jeremiah 7:9; 22:6-12; Matthew 5:3-10; Romans 1:24-32; 1 Corinthians 5:9-11; 6:9-10; Galatians 5:19-20,22-23; Ephesians 4:31-32; 5:3-4; Philippians 4:8; Colossians 3:5-9,12-14; 2 Timothy 3:2-5; James 3:17; 1 Peter 4:3; Revelation 9:20-21.

What vices/sins did you notice over and over again?

What virtues/godly characteristics did you notice over and over again?

What personal weaknesses did you notice in the vice categories, and what personal, God-given strengths did you notice in the virtue categories?

If you haven't already done so, please consider watching (or if it's been awhile, rewatching!) with friends and family the movie *Amazing Grace*. This film tells of William Wilberforce's crusade to abolish slavery. Afterward, loiter over coffee and dessert to discuss what you could do to promote social justice in your corner of the world, and in so doing glorify God.

# Wonderful, Weighty Words

The following theological terms can help you better comprehend and communicate the *how much more* aspect of God's love, or, at the very least, help you impress folks at future dinner parties!

**EXEGESIS:** critical explanation or interpretation of a text or portion of a text, especially of the Bible; typically deals with both the grammar and syntax of the original biblical languages of Hebrew, Greek, and Aramaic.[4]

**HERMENEUTICS:** the science of interpretation, especially of the Scriptures; the branch of theology that deals with the principles of biblical exegesis.[5]

**INERRANCY:** Wayne Grudem says "The inerrancy of Scripture means that Scripture in the original manuscripts does not affirm anything that is contrary to the fact."[6] In other words, the Bible always tells the truth and is inerrant for God's intended purposes.

**STATIC HERMENEUTIC:** The study of Scripture "which understands the words of the text aside from or with minimal emphasis upon their underlying spirit and thus restricts any modern application of Scripture to where the isolated words of the text fell in their original setting."[7]

**REDEMPTIVE MOVEMENT HERMENEUTIC:** The study of Scripture "which encourages movement beyond the original application of the text in the ancient world" and captures the redemptive movement within Scripture.[8]

# How Much More

## REDEMPTIVE IS GOD'S UNCONDITIONAL LOVE

When the LORD first spoke to Hosea,
he said this to him:
Go and marry a woman of promiscuity,
and have children of promiscuity,
for the land is committing blatant acts of promiscuity
by abandoning the LORD.
So he went and married Gomer daughter of Diblaim,
and she conceived and bore him a son.

**HOSEA 1:2-3**

## Session Three: ALL IT TOOK WAS JUST ONE LOOK

To access the video teaching sessions, use the
instructions in the back of your Bible study book.

## DISCUSSION QUESTIONS

What impacted you the most from the video teaching?

Have you ever done a study or heard teaching on the Song of Songs? What was the context? What did you learn?

Do you ever settle for mediocrity in your relationship with God? Explain.

How does the story from the Song of Songs help you better understand God's love for you?

Do you feel you are able to bring all of yourself to God? If not, what seems to hold you back the most from an intimate relationship with Him?

How would truly understanding the extravagant love God has for you change your relationship with Him and change the way you live your life?

How did this video teaching reveal the redemptive heart and extravagant love of God?

# Stretching Sacred Muscles

When it comes to romance, my life tends to be either a blooper reel or a desert, depending on the season. Now that I'm in my fifties, I've had enough Christian counseling to understand my dearth of dating relationships stems from my fear of intimacy, which was instilled at an early age. My Dad Harper left us when I was five years old to start another life with a new wife and her young son. During the years that passed between my parents' acrimonious divorce and my mom's remarriage, I was sexually molested by several adult men posing as friendly "uncles," supposedly trying to help our little family navigate the aftermath of said divorce. Then I was date-raped in college. Suffice it to say, intimacy—especially intimacy with men in a romantic context—wasn't my strong suit. It took decades for me to recognize that I'd subconsciously stiff-armed God as a result.

I was pretty comfortable with the idea of Him as the King of all kings and Lord of all lords, but the concept of Jesus as the Lover of my soul was disconcerting. As I explained in the last video teaching session on the Song of Songs, I just couldn't imagine God gazing at me affectionately and saying, "You have captured my heart with one glance of your eyes" (Song of Sg. 4:9b). The *how much more* reality of God's love for me never quite made it to the center of my heart. It kept getting hung up on the jagged-edged scars of abuse that still riddled my mind.

> Read Isaiah 54:5. Which facet of God are you more comfortable with—the fact that He's our Maker/Creator or that He's our heavenly husband. Explain your answer.

> Reread Song of Songs 4:9. When you picture yourself standing in the affectionate gaze of God, what is your initial reaction? Can you identify any "jagged-edged" remainders from your past that make it more difficult for you to lean into the intimate affection He has for you now? Have you ever felt "kissed" by God? If so, describe the circumstances that surrounded that holy, proverbial smooch.

Read Exodus 26:31-37; 1 Timothy 6:15; and Revelation 19:16.

The same Hebrew idiom used to express the superlative in phrases like "the most holy place," "the Lord of lords," or "the King of kings" (i.e., "the best of the best"), is used to describe the Song of Songs.

> In light of the fact that there are lots of other significant songs in the Bible, including Moses' song in Exodus 15, Deborah's song in Judges 5, Hannah's song in 1 Samuel 2, Mary's song—the *Magnificat*—at the beginning of the Gospel of Luke (1:46-55), plus all 150 psalms, which were originally written as songs, why do you think God titled this particular, rather explicit Old Testament tune as the most excellent of all?

As an obvious slow learner when it comes to leaning fully into the divine intimacy God has made available to us in Christ, I'm so grateful for His promise in Philippians: "I am sure of this, that he who started a good work in you will carry it on to completion until the day of Christ Jesus" (1:6).

That basically means that despite how dim-witted I can be regarding the *how much more* facets of His love, God won't let me miss it! Which explains why during the same season I was neck-deep in the Song of Songs, the Holy Spirit prompted me to peruse another wild biblical romance—the one between a good guy named Hosea and a naughty girl named Gomer.

Hosea is the first of nine **PREEXILIC** books in a twelve-book section located at the very end of the Old Testament, commonly called the Minor Prophets. (The last three books are **POSTEXILIC**.) I used to think they were called "minor" because the gentlemen who wrote them were on Keto and therefore waifish dudes who wore skinny jeans like most of the baristas in Nashville. But that's not the case at all. The twelve tomes which make up the caboose section of the Old Testament are designated as minor because they're relatively short books, unlike the prophecies given by Isaiah and Jeremiah. However, despite their brevity— none of the Minor Prophets is more than a few chapters in length—every single one is filled with passion, intrigue, and unforgettable images of God.

# Part of Israel's History

Take a few moments to peruse some of the happenings in the story of the nation of Israel while the books in the Minor Prophets were being written.[1]

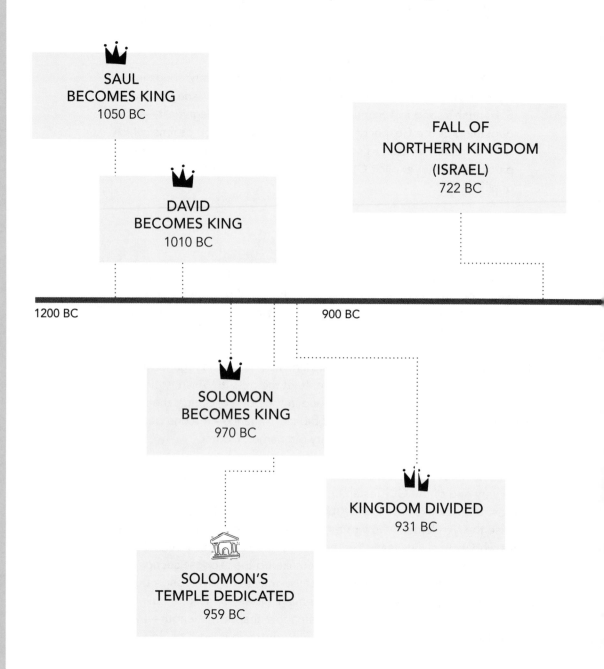

SAUL
BECOMES KING
1050 BC

DAVID
BECOMES KING
1010 BC

FALL OF
NORTHERN KINGDOM
(ISRAEL)
722 BC

1200 BC

900 BC

SOLOMON
BECOMES KING
970 BC

KINGDOM DIVIDED
931 BC

SOLOMON'S
TEMPLE DEDICATED
959 BC

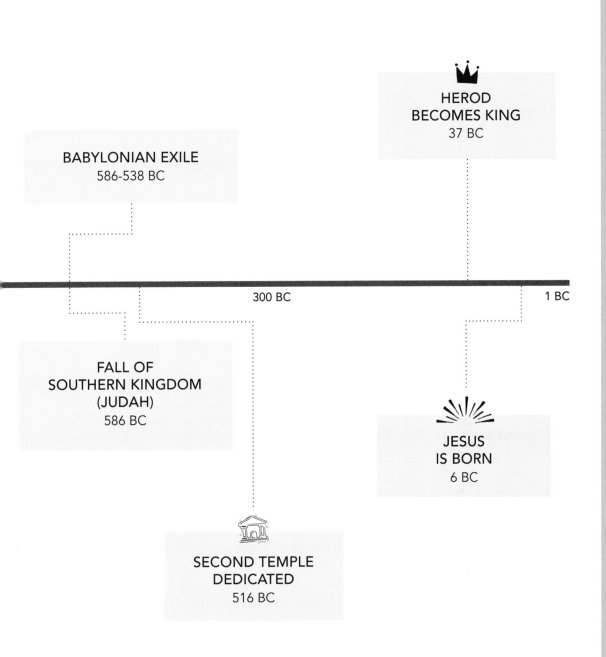

BABYLONIAN EXILE
586-538 BC

HEROD
BECOMES KING
37 BC

300 BC

1 BC

FALL OF
SOUTHERN KINGDOM
(JUDAH)
586 BC

JESUS
IS BORN
6 BC

SECOND TEMPLE
DEDICATED
516 BC

The Minor Prophets were written over a span of about four hundred years (from 835 BC to 432 BC).[2] And those four hundred years represent an extremely tumultuous time in Israel's history. They were in turmoil partly because of bad leadership. After forty years of strong leadership, King David died, leaving the keys to the throne to his smart son, Solomon. And while Solomon was a brilliant, very literary king (he wrote most of Proverbs and possibly some of the other wisdom books), he flunked the final exam of leadership because, like me (and probably more than a few of you), he had intimacy issues. This became glaringly apparent after the applause-worthy early years of his reign—characterized by following in his dad's footsteps in obedience to God—when he evidently got bored with the Shulammite woman from the Song of Songs and went on a reckless acquiring-more-spouses spree.

Solomon became a total player, eventually accruing seven hundred wives and three hundred concubines (1 Kings 11:1-3). I suppose dealing with all of that competing estrogen in the palace fried his brain because he ended up following his pagan wives into idol worship (vv. 4-8). As you can imagine, this didn't sit well with the Lord. He was angry with Solomon and declared that because of the king's disobedience, He would "tear the kingdom away" from Solomon and give it to someone else (v. 11). But for David's sake, God declared this reckoning would not take place during Solomon's reign; rather, it would come to pass after Solomon's son took power. And the kingdom would be split, not totally torn from the family (vv. 9-13). That's exactly what happened. After Solomon's son Rehoboam became king, the kingdom divided, north and south (12:1-19).

The Northern Kingdom retained the name Israel. The Southern Kingdom became known as Judah, which boasted beautiful Jerusalem—the "City of God" (Ps. 46:4)—as its capital. The fallout of this kingdom divide was God's people began warring amongst themselves as often as they fought against foreign nations. Unfortunately, all that inner havoc distracted them from trusting in God as their sovereign leader and drove them to make foolhardy alliances with former enemies like Assyria in a dangerous game of political roulette.

As a result of cozying up to people they used to cross swords with, God's people also swung the door to their sanctuary wide open, allowing other religions to waltz into their once monotheistic way of life. Instead of being one nation under God, Israel became a crazy, compromised, spiritual smorgasbord. Much like Charles Dickens' opening line in A Tale of Two Cities, "It was the best of times, it was the worst of times" in the land of milk and honey.[3] To some it initially appeared to be the best because the national economy was thriving, and they were experiencing unprecedented favor with surrounding nations. But it turned out to be the worst. God's chosen people—specially selected to be a theocracy representing the kind of loving, "monogamous" relationship He'd designed for humanity to experience with Him—were turning their backs on Him. They were spending much more time at the mall than at church. They were frolicking in their newfound material excess and flinging loyalty to Jehovah out the window. Hedonism replaced holiness. Needless to say, when Solomon went looking for love in all the wrong places, he brought the whole country down with him.

It would be perfectly understandable if God had chosen to fry the whole lot of them into grease spots of oblivion and fashion another, more faithful theocracy out of a less turbulent tribe … but He didn't. Instead, He picked an honorable prophet named Hosea from relative obscurity and told him to marry the sleaziest girl in town. Then, through that unlikeliest of love stories, our Creator Redeemer reminded His prone-to-wander people *how much more* His love for them is worth than the cheap, dime-store baubles they'd become infatuated with.

> Read 1 Kings 11:9-13. In light of this passage, how would you describe the relationship between godly ancestry and God's mercy? Are there any Christians in your family history? If so, how have their testimonies affected your walk of faith?

> Read Psalm 84:11. What encouragement does this promise give you regarding things you don't understand about God or places where you haven't fully trusted Him yet?

> Read 1 Timothy 3:1-5,8-12. Why do you think God included being a good father in the list of qualifications for church leadership? What parenting characteristics do you think best correlate with spiritual maturity?

# Learning Redemptive Rhythms

According to Hosea 1:1, the prophet Hosea preached during the reigns of four successive kings of Judah (a span of about fifty years in 8th century B.C.), and his name literally means "salvation" in Hebrew.[4] Other than that, all we know about him comes from the poignant story God asked him to live and record. Thus, in the absence of knowable details, I'm going to use considerable creative license to describe what Hosea might have been like. Since he was a prophet and therefore an all-around good guy, I picture him wearing high-water khakis, a short-sleeved white button-down shirt with a tie his grandmother gave him for his *bar mitzvah*, New Balance running shoes, and thick glasses. He was the vice-president of his high school math club, took stats for the football team, and was a loyal member of the F.P.S.—the Future Prophets Society. What he wasn't was the type of guy who posted pictures of his abs on social media or texted off-color requests to tacky girls. Frankly, Hosea probably wasn't the type of guy who dated that much. My guess is he was too shy to ask a girl to prom and far too virtuous to ask one to make out in the back seat of his parents' car.

In light of Hosea's wholesome status, he must've been stunned at God's request:

> The first time GOD spoke to Hosea he said:
> "Find a whore and marry her.
> Make this whore the mother of your children.
> And here's why: This whole country
> has become a whorehouse, unfaithful to me, GOD."

**HOSEA 1:2, MSG**

Yikers. I bet Hosea's face turned bright red before God even completed His command. I also bet Hosea knew exactly which girl God was talking about. First of all, the kingdom wasn't that big. And secondly, Gomer's name was scribbled all over the boys locker room. Lots of guys knew Gomer, if you catch my drift. And it was her immoral behavior that made her the perfect metaphor for God's chosen people. They had a pretty racy reputation too. They'd betrayed the Creator of the universe for meaningless flings with idols and had numerous affairs with false prophets. Faithfulness wasn't their forte.

But what shocked me most when I first began holding this diamond of a true tale up to the light to admire its facets wasn't Gomer's decadence, it was

Hosea's obedience. I found myself gaping in amazement over the fact that Hosea didn't protest. He didn't put his hands on his hips, look toward the heavens with indignation, then stomp off in an offended huff. He didn't even quibble, which would've made total sense, humanly speaking. I mean, it sounds reasonable to me if some pious dude balked when asked to marry the town floozy. But Hosea didn't. In the English Standard Version, Hosea 1:3 begins simply with, "So he went …"

> Sit quietly for a moment and reflect on what God was asking Hosea to do in Hosea 1:2. Consider your willingness and desire to obey God in all things. Would your willingness stand or wilt if called to obey what might seem to you to be an unfair, outlandish command? Explain.

I don't know about you, but when God asks me to do something difficult and I do what He says, I typically expect a good return on my investment. Especially if it costs me personal inconvenience or emotional pain. For instance, not too long ago I was given too much change at a fast food drive-through window. When I realized I'd been given change based on $20 instead of the $10 I'd actually handed the cashier, I turned my car around, parked, and went into the restaurant to give the extra money back. I was in a big hurry and didn't really have the time to go inside (which is why I was picking up greasy food from a drive-through in the first place!), but I didn't want anyone to get in trouble when they came up $10 short at the end of the day. Plus, God's Word is pretty clear when it comes to honesty.

However, when I took the time to go inside and explain the situation to the cashier, you would've thought I'd passed her a note that said, "This is a stickup and I'm wearing Depends." She seemed alarmed and disgusted at the same time. Then she sighed in exasperation and told me to wait because she was going to have to get the assistant manager in order to straighten things out. The situation didn't get much better with him. He told me that this whole customer-returning-cash thing wasn't covered in their training manual, and he didn't know how to put money back into the register without some type of transaction. I explained that I was just trying to do the right thing, and he gave me the now familiar alarmed/disgusted look.

I ended up leaving the money on the counter and walking out of the restaurant with several pairs of eyes watching me warily. I didn't expect a parade or an Instagram story praising my integrity, but I didn't expect to be treated like a nutjob either. The older I get, the more I'm learning that spiritual obedience is rarely congruent with what our culture calls logical. And God's pleasure rarely presents itself with public fanfare.

Read 1 Corinthians 1:26-31. How can recognizing our own weakness and incapacities actually help us see God's love exponentially bigger and clearer?

Many people have questioned why God would ask one of His children to marry a woman He knew would commit adultery. If you had to write a paper or engage in a debate on this subject, how would you justify God asking Hosea to marry a "whore"? What's the most difficult thing you've sensed God asking you to do recently?

Read Exodus 34:14-16; Isaiah 62:5; and Jeremiah 3:14. How does our relationship with God differ from a human husband and wife relationship? In what ways do you think it's similar?

In my imagination, "So he went ..." (Hos. 1:3a) is followed by Hosea heading to the bank, cashing out all the hard-earned money he'd made working for Amazon during a global pandemic, and driving to the mall and buying the biggest diamond chip of an engagement ring he could afford. Then he drives home, showers and shaves, puts on his one and only suit, sloshes on the cologne his favorite aunt had given him for Hanukkah, gets in his beat-up, used Prius, and heads to Gomer's house. I can picture him nervously walking up to the doorstep and courteously knocking on the door. My guess is that Mr. Diblaim's watching a ball game with the volume turned up so loud that he doesn't hear Hosea knocking until he resorts to pounding. And when Mr. D reluctantly puts down his Bud Light, hoists himself out of his tattered recliner, clomps to the door and flings it open, he finds a sheepish looking, clean-cut young man who reeks of cologne standing there with a fistful of red roses. Diblaim thinks he must've guzzled so much beer that he's hallucinating, because clean-cut young men are about as common in their neighborhood as winning the lottery.

But then Hosea's voice cuts through his stupor: "Good evening, Mr. Diblaim. My name is Hosea Good Guy, and I'm here because I want to ask your daughter Gomer to marry me, and I'd like your blessing."

Surely Diblaim's inebriated guffaws can be heard for blocks.

"*Are you punkin' me, boy?* Got one of your buddies hiding somewhere with a GoPro filming all this?"

When Diblaim finally quits laughing and realizes Hosea is serious, he bellows for Gomer. She hollers back, "Whatchu want, Daddy?" because what with the heavy metal music thumping through her earbuds, she can't hear him very well. When she pokes her head out of her room to find out what all the commotion is about, she sees Hosea standing politely in their doorway holding a small bouquet of wilting roses. She recognizes him immediately. The academic dean at their high school had assigned him to be her Algebra 2 peer tutor the previous semester. She flushes at the thought, remembering how she pulled the neckline of her shirt even lower than usual before meeting him, assuming he'd eventually give in to her flirtations like all the other boys. But he never did. He never looked at her chest while explaining algorithms in the library and always greeted her courteously in the hallways.

After an awkward few seconds of staring, Gomer moves to the door and recovers her self-protective veneer of detached sarcasm. She asks, "What're you doing slumming in our neighborhood, Hose? Selling magazines for the Boy Scouts or something?" In response he drops to one knee, takes one of her hands gently in his while placing a velvet ring box in her other hand, then looks directly into her eyes and proclaims sincerely, "God sent me here to ask you to marry me, Gomer. Will you please do me the honor of becoming my wife?" At which point she has to bite her lip to keep from crying. She's never had anyone speak to her with such kind consideration. She and her daddy are both shocked when the words, "Sure, why not?" fall out of her mouth. Within an hour the whole town is stunned because news of their engagement has started trending on Twitter.

Can't you picture them getting married in a small ceremony—him in a borrowed tux and her in a tight dress, wearing way too much blue eye shadow? Going on a short honeymoon and then settling in a modest two-bed, one-bath apartment? I imagine Hosea working hard at an entry-level temple job, determined to provide well for their little family, and Gomer trying to act like an appropriate suburban housewife, exchanging her crop tops for cardigans.

Based on their divergent backgrounds, Gomer was probably appreciative of Hosea's thoughtfulness at first. The way he always called to let her know if he'd be home late from work. The way he always opened her car door first before walking around to get in on the other side. Monogamy brought with it an unfamiliar, yet wonderful feeling of security. Maybe he even surprised her on their first anniversary with the keys to a cute little brick bungalow. By then he'd probably landed a preaching job with a pension and she'd joined a book club. They had two children, a boy named Jezreel and a girl named Lo-ruhamah (Hos. 1:4-6) and bought a minivan. But just when everyone assumed Gomer's promiscuity was history and Hosea didn't get such a bad deal after all, she got pregnant again, and this time she lived up to her former reputation.

> After Gomer had weaned Lo-ruhamah, she again became pregnant and gave birth to a second son. And the Lord said, "Name him Lo-ammi—'Not my people'—for Israel is not my people, and I am not their God."

### HOSEA 1:8-9, NLT

This basically meant God was fed up with His people's disobedience. It also meant the third child bore no resemblance whatsoever to Hosea, which must've felt like a knife had been driven deeply into his tender heart.

Read Genesis 2:18-25; Exodus 3:13-15; and Philippians 2:1-11. Biblical narrative makes it clear that there was a sacred element when it came to someone's name. What's the genesis of your name, and how did your parents choose it?

Read Hosea 1:6 and Psalm 136. How do you reconcile the prophetic doom in Gomer and Hosea's little girl's name with the promise that God's love endures forever in Psalm 136? Do you think God ever truly abandons His people?

Read Psalm 51. The context of this psalm is King David's confession for committing adultery with Bathsheba, yet in verse 4 he says: "Against you—you alone—I have sinned and done this evil in your sight," referring specifically to God. What does that imply about sin? What would you say are similar consequences of marital adultery and spiritual adultery (i.e., worshiping something/someone other than God)?

# Following God's Lead

After saddling Gomer and Hosea's three children with soberly prophetic forenames, God paints a vivid picture of Gomer's—and metaphorically His people's—indiscretions:

> Yes, their mother is promiscuous; she conceived them and acted shamefully. For she thought, "I will follow my lovers,the men who give me my food and water, my wool and flax, my oil and drink."

**HOSEA 2:5**

In modern context, Gomer went bar hopping while Hosea stayed home and played single parent to their three young children. He drove carpool, packed their sack lunches, helped them with their homework, put Band-Aids on their scraped knees, and did all the cooking and the laundry. He's also the one who haltingly led Lo-ruhamah down the feminine hygiene aisle at Walmart when she turned twelve and explained puberty as best he could, stammering sweetly the whole time. All the while their momma was making out with traveling salesmen who plied her with cheap jewelry and piña coladas.

The most painful memories in my life are being left by my father and having to leave Missy at the orphanage in Haiti. It still grieves me deeply to remember how she wailed mournfully and begged me to not to leave her. She was too little to comprehend that in order to legally finalize the adoption I had to go back to America, but that I would keep coming back to be with her for as long as it took until I could bring her home to Tennessee. And if the legal route failed, I was committed to move to Haiti to be with her. I can't imagine willingly abandoning my daughter.

The last ten verses of Hosea 2 describe God's mercy for His people in spite of how they've prostituted their affections. It's a beautifully redemptive passage that begins with God's promise to allure Israel on a trip into the wilderness (v. 14). Then He refers to the sweet things He's going to say to His beloved there. But as much as I relish the idea of a special date night in the country with our Creator, it's the last three verses of this chapter that draw me in the most. That's when our gracious heavenly Father turns His attention back to those two little boys and the little girl who were devastated when their mama bounced:

"On the very same day, I'll answer"—this is GOD's Message—"I'll answer the sky, sky will answer earth, Earth will answer grain and wine and olive oil, and they'll all answer Jezreel. I'll plant her in the good earth. I'll have mercy on No-Mercy. I'll say to Nobody, 'You're my dear Somebody,' and he'll say 'You're my God!'"

### HOSEA 2:21-23, MSG

Of course, Scripture doesn't specify how Hosea's kids felt about their birth names. Perhaps they were too little to understand the prophetic connotation. But I'll bet they held their heads higher and sat straighter and maybe even hid shy smiles behind their hands when the schoolteacher called out their new names the next morning at roll call!

My first real boyfriend was a catch named Keith. We started "going together" in the eighth grade. The first gift he gave me to celebrate our serious case of puppy love was a gold ID bracelet with his name inscribed on it in big, block letters. I was so proud of that bracelet. I didn't care one bit that it turned my arm green! When God chooses to circle back to these three, wounded kids and redeem their slur names, He recognizes them as belonging to Him. He essentially gives them His ID bracelet, confirming, "These little ones are Mine." Never forget that the omnipotent Creator of the universe is also a tenderhearted Daddy who is fiercely possessive and protective of His children.

With that in mind, I invite you once again to find a relatively quiet place where you can be alone for at least ten minutes. Then open your Bible and read Hosea 1:2-9; 2:14-20. Talk to God about where you've looked for love in all the wrong places. Tell Him when you've struggled to really lean into His embrace and let Him hold you. Confess where you may still have jagged edges of fear, unforgiveness, or unbelief that keep you from fully receiving and resting in His love for you. Ask Him to give you the grace to lift your head and look into His radiant countenance while He gazes at you affectionately and says, "You have captured my heart with one glance of your eyes" (Song of Sg. 4:9b).

If you're comfortable doing so, feel free to use the lines below to journal your prayers and how you sense the Holy Spirit guiding you with regard to experiencing more intimacy in your relationship with God.

Now read Hosea 2:21-23; Isaiah 43:1-4; 62:4-5; John 15:12-15; and Galatians 4:4-7. Write a responsive prayer in the space below about the old "slur names" you've been saddled with in the past and the new, redemptive names God has given you to wear from this day forward.

DEAR JESUS, THESE ARE THE SLUR-NAMES I'VE WORN IN MY PAST AND THE LIES I BELIEVED ABOUT MYSELF WHILE WEARING THEM:

DEAR JESUS, THESE ARE THE NEW NAMES ACCORDING TO YOUR PROMISES THAT I GET TO BE DEFINED BY NOW:

DEAR JESUS, THESE ARE THINGS/VOICES/RELATIONSHIPS THAT TEMPT ME TO TURN AWAY FROM YOU AND COMMIT SPIRITUAL ADULTERY. PLEASE FORGIVE ME AND HELP ME STAY FAITHFUL TO YOU:

# Dancing For Good

The final scene recorded in Hosea and Gomer's unlikely love story is incredible to the point of being incredulous, because their epic estrangement ends at a slave market. You see, Gomer's adultery had at least metaphorically spiraled her downward towards prostitution, and when other men stopped paying for her dinner, liquor, and living expenses like "food and water, ... clothing of wool and linen, and ... olive oil and drinks" (2:5b, NLT), she started selling her body to pay the bills. Then it seems, from Hosea's need to buy her back (3:2), that when that "business" began waning, Gomer felt forced to sell herself off as a slave.

As dramatic as this Old Testament descent into debauchery may seem, I can tell you I've witnessed many similar distressing stories firsthand through a faith-based, addiction recovery ministry I volunteer with that helps get women like Gomer off the streets. Over the years I've gotten to know quite a few "former Gomers," and every single one whom I've had the privilege of befriending never planned to go into what's often referred to as "the world's oldest profession." My friends at the ministry didn't ask for prostitute Barbies® for Christmas when they were little girls. More often than not, they were sexually abused as children. And those first, filthy handprints that marred the precious cement of their innocent hearts led them to believe they were dirty and damaged and didn't deserve to be loved.

What I've often witnessed in ministerial settings—and for many years what I experienced personally—is the trajectory of a life that encounters abuse early on ends up bending toward self-destruction. Abuse victims tend to have heart-breakingly precocious capacities for numbing pain. Maybe it starts out looking innocuous enough—like a vivacious cheerleader who drinks a bit too much after ball games. But then it all goes downhill from there when that same, seemingly bubbly girl starts getting blackout drunk several times a week and ends up having one night stands with most of the football team before she even qualifies for a driver's license. She drops out of school at the end of her junior year, develops a meth habit, gets seduced by a thirty-something-year-old pimp who masquerades as an empathetic, mature boyfriend, and ends up getting arrested for solicitation the very same month she should've been graduating from high school. (This is the actual decline of one of the lovely young women I met soon after her arrest and quickly became very fond of. She's now been sober for a decade, is happily married, and runs a nonprofit that helps others break free from the bondage of addiction.)

As offensive as Gomer's behavior initially seems, I can't help but wonder what happened to her when she was a little girl, before everyone in town branded her a whore, long before she accepted Hosea's outlandish marriage proposal. I find myself still pondering what the genesis of her pain was. What led to the straw that broke her? What pushed her to the point where she felt like she had no option but to sell herself into slavery, then bottomed out on an auction block?

Read Romans 5:8. What was the condition of your life when you first began to believe that God loved you? What part of "still" left the largest scars on your heart and mind?

Read James 1:12-16. Has there been a season in your life in which temptation has given way to sin, which then spiraled out of control? If so, how? More importantly, how did God help you off the proverbial auctioneer's block you'd climbed up on when, like dear Gomer, you didn't see another way out of your self-destructive spiral?

Read Hosea 2:6-7. Looking back on your life, can you now see a season in which God built some type of hedge around you to keep you from making more bad decisions and ultimately doing even more damage to yourself or others? Did you recognize that it was His merciful protection at the time? If so, how?

Historical accounts reveal atrocious details about ancient slave markets where slaves were stripped bare and placed on boulders or small pillars so that potential buyers could "examine the merchandise." I hesitate to imagine the lewd comments men made as they scrutinized and groped poor Gomer. Perhaps an old drinking buddy of hers cackled derisively before bragging loudly, "Why should I pay for something I've already had for free?" Or maybe a lecherous stranger asked boldly, "Can I sample this here slave before deciding whether or not I want to buy her?" All the while Gomer had to stand there silently and submissively, probably staring at her feet with tears streaming down her face and wishing she could go back in time and change the choices that led to this living hell. Or perhaps wishing she could just die and get it over with.

But then she hears a familiar voice. A clear, clarion call over the raucous crowd, "I want to buy that beautiful woman, and I'll give you more than what you're asking!" She looks up to see Hosea, the doting husband she'd abandoned years before. He's standing there in his best suit, wearing a compassionate expression. She can scarcely believe it's him. It's been so long. She notices he's got a little grey in his hair now and then guiltily realizes how many years have passed since she's seen him or the children. Yet there he is, handing the auctioneer a money order and grinning from ear to ear like some lucky commoner who won a date with a gorgeous princess.

According to Old Testament Law and Jewish tradition, Hosea had the legal right to have Gomer put to death for her sexual indiscretions (Lev. 20:10). He could've been standing there with a couple of burly policemen, prepared to give his unfaithful wife a speedy trial and capital punishment. But he's not there for vengeance. He'd taken money out of his retirement account and hopped on the first flight he could get to be at that terrible auction for mercy's sake. He didn't push through that rough crowd of beer-chugging, dirty-joke-telling hooligans to retaliate against his adulterous wife but to redeem her.

Don't you wish you had a YouTube video of this moment? I bet Gomer's mouth fell open with shock when Hosea reached up and gently took one of her hands in his—just like he'd done all those years ago in her parents' doorway—and then said lovingly, "Come on, Honey, it's time to go home."

> Then the Lord said to me, "Go, and get your wife again
> and bring her back to you and love her, even though she
> loves adultery. For the Lord still loves Israel though she has

turned to other gods and offered them choice gifts."
So I bought her back from her slavery for a couple of
dollars and eight bushels of barley, and I said to her, "You
must live alone for many days; do not go out with other
men nor be a prostitute, and I will wait for you."

### HOSEA 3:1-3, TLB

We mustn't forget the symbolism of this minor prophet's marriage. God told Hosea to propose to Gomer because her unfaithfulness would be the perfect metaphor for the way His people were abandoning their faith. God used an appalling betrayal—a loose woman abandoning both her loving husband and children—to snag the attention of His idolatrous people. To warn them about the consequences of spiritual adultery and to woo them back to Himself with an unforgettable story about how divine love is infinitely better than prone-to-wander people like them—and us—think we deserve. If you've ever wondered what biblical scene best illustrates God's *how much more* love for us, apart from our Savior on the cross, you don't have to look any further than Hosea barging into that slave market, striding through that crowd of boisterous bidders, and buying back his estranged wife.

One of the best dancing for good moves we can make in light of this story is to never forget the Gomer aspect of our own story, which will compel us to love Jesus our Redeemer more and judge other mistake-prone people less.

> Review Hosea 3:1-3 and read Numbers 5:11-15. The amount Hosea paid for Gomer was fifteen shekels of silver and approximately nine bushels of barley. It's possible this added up to the going rate for a slave, which was thirty shekels of silver (Ex. 21:32)—the same amount Judas was paid to betray Jesus. What insight can you draw from Numbers 5:11-15 regarding why God specified for Hosea to buy Gomer back with silver and grain?

In light of the fact that Numbers 5:11-15 explains that a grain offering pertains to a husband's jealousy over his wife's unfaithfulness, my opinion is that God prompted Hosea to offer those bushels of barley to ensure that he wouldn't rub Gomer's nose in her guilty past at any point during the future of their now-restored marriage relationship. In other words, the stain of her adultery had been completely erased, never to be mentioned again!

Has someone ever paid off a significant debt on your behalf (i.e., your parents paying off your student loan or an out-of-control credit card balance)? If so, how did it make you feel?

Read Luke 7:36-50. How has your awareness of the egregious nature of your own sin developed since you began your walk of faith? How would you describe the relationship between your intimacy with Jesus and that awareness?

The thread that runs through all fourteen chapters of Hosea is God's affection for His undeserving people. Despite our dirty and oft-divided hearts, He loves us more than we can possibly imagine. Read Hosea 14:9; Psalm 107:43; and Ecclesiastes 12:13-14. How would you synopsize the promise these verses proclaim?

# Wonderful, Weighty Words

The following theological terms can help you better comprehend and communicate the *how much more* aspect of God's love, or, at the very least, help you impress folks at future dinner parties!

**THEOCRACY:** a nation or people group specially chosen by God to represent a covenant relationship with Him. And while the Jewish nation is the theocracy our Creator Redeemer established in the Old Testament, I firmly believe their covenant status is illustrative of His desire to have a personal relationship with all of His image bearers.

**PREEXILIC:** Relating to the period or events before the exile (before 587 B.C.).[5]

**POSTEXILIC:** Relating to the period or events following Israel's Babylonian exile (after 539 B.C.).[6]

## Extra Credit Biblical History Information For Inquiring Minds:

The historical notation "BC" stands for "before Christ" and represents the time period preceding Jesus' birth. AD is a historical abbreviation for the Latin words *anno Domini*, which translated means "the year of our Lord" and represents the time period after Jesus was born (a common misconception is that AD stands for "after His death"). Those two notations—BC and AD—have been used worldwide for well over a thousand years to designate the time periods before and after the birth of Jesus Christ. However, the notations BCE and CE, are quickly replacing them in modernity. BCE stands for "before the common era" and CE stands for "common era." They essentially have the same type of dating reference and application but have effectively removed God from how human-kind frames history. For obvious reasons, I still prefer the old-school BC and AD notations.

# How Much More

## SHOULD THE GOSPEL WE PROCLAIM BRING HOPE TO OUR BROKEN WORLD

At that time the kingdom of heaven will be like ten virgins who took their lamps and went out to meet the groom. Five of them were foolish and five were wise. When the foolish took their lamps, they didn't take oil with them; but the wise ones took oil in their flasks with their lamps. When the groom was delayed, they all became drowsy and fell asleep. In the middle of the night there was a shout: "Here's the groom! Come out to meet him." Then all the virgins got up and trimmed their lamps. The foolish ones said to the wise ones, "Give us some of your oil, because our lamps are going out." The wise ones answered, "No, there won't be enough for us and for you. Go instead to those who sell oil, and buy some for yourselves." When they had gone to buy some, the groom arrived, and those who were ready went in with him to the wedding banquet, and the door was shut. Later the rest of the virgins also came and said, "Master, master, open up for us!" He replied, "Truly I tell you, I don't know you!" Therefore be alert, because you don't know either the day or the hour.

## MATTHEW 25:1-13

# Session Four: HIS SUPERNATURAL, SUPERLATIVE AFFECTION

To access the video teaching sessions, use the instructions in the back of your Bible study book.

## DISCUSSION QUESTIONS

What impacted you the most from the video teaching?

What causes us to view the Bible as more of a rule book rather than a love story? Has this been your experience? Explain.

How does the gospel stand in opposition to our current culture? Is this surprising to you? Explain.

How have you personally faced opposition for the sake of the gospel?

Do you shamelessly and boldly present your requests to God? What keeps you from praying audacious prayers?

What are some bold prayers you've seen God answer in your life, your family, or your church? What audacious things are you currently asking God for?

How did this video teaching reveal the redemptive heart and extravagant love of God?

# Stretching Sacred Muscles

My first foray into teaching the Bible was in high school when my best friend, Cindy, and I started a weekly study through the Fellowship of Christian Athletes. We were wildly enthusiastic about sharing the gospel, probably a tad heretical in our exegesis, and definitely delighted that most of the football team chose to be in FCA! And it's in that context that I first seriously pondered the idea of adoption, prompted by our teaching a study on the theme of adoption in Scripture. Soon following that study, Cindy and I both soberly vowed to adopt orphaned children when we grew up and got married. Cindy married soon after graduating from college, and not long afterward she and her husband, Peter, adopted Michael, and then several years later adopted Ivy.

Meanwhile, I was one of those "always the bridesmaid, never the bride" kind of girls who threw myself into youth ministry, followed by a long, mostly wonderful stint at a large Christian organization where pantyhose were part of the dress code for female staffers. Plus, we weren't allowed to wear open-toed shoes because someone in leadership was convinced that the line between a woman's big toe and second toe resembled cleavage and could cause men to have lustful thoughts. Therefore, I sacrificed a large part of my thirties to an uncomfortable, yet chaste, fog.

Shortly before turning forty I moved to Nashville to work on a church staff and attend seminary. I soon attended what proved to be a life-changing breakout session at a women's conference. I chose that particular breakout session because of the emphasis on missions, so I was thrown off guard when the facilitator began talking about adoption. She announced that there are 147 million orphans in the world today (this number fluctuates from year to year but has been well over 100 million for a very long time), many of whom are languishing in Third World countries with little hope of surviving infancy because of easily preventable diseases like malaria, cholera, tuberculosis, and challenging conditions like widespread malnutrition. Then she quoted that familiar verse in James about how taking care of widows and orphans is our responsibility as followers of Christ, after which she paused for a long moment—looking many of us directly in the eyes—before asking intently, "What are you doing about it?"

I can still remember the conviction that reverberated through the room and through my spirit that Saturday afternoon almost twenty years ago. I wasn't sure how to answer her question, because, as a forty-year-old single woman from a conservative theological background, I wasn't sure I was even allowed to adopt a child. I mean, good night, I'd just begun to exercise the liberty of leaving the house without pantyhose! But I couldn't shake the feeling that God was calling me to do something involving orphan care, like maybe take a sabbatical to spend time volunteering in an orphanage or make more of a financial investment in those kinds of ministries. So I decided to share my conviciton with four girls from a Bible study small group I was engaged in and ask them to pray for me to be able to better discern God's direction.

Three of those small group friends essentially said, "We've got your back and will pray with you and for you." But one said, "If you've got time later on this week, I'd like to meet you for coffee and process your prayer request about adoption a little further."

(Now this has nothing to do with the passage we're about to peruse; however, it may be a redemptive rabbit trail to warn you about the potential danger of pew-warming Pharisees. Suffice it to say, if a woman wearing a fake smile tells you that she has a "word from the Lord" she needs to share with you in private, my strong encouragement is to play dumb and take a friend.)

Unfortunately, I've never been the sharpest tool in the shed when it comes to recognizing shame mongers masquerading as prophets, so I met with her by myself at Starbucks. At which point she said, "Lisa, I want to be very straightforward about your prayer request regarding the issue of adoption, because the Bible says the wounds of a friend are better than the kiss of an enemy (Prov. 27:6). I do not think you're a good candidate for motherhood because of the sexual abuse you told us you experienced when you were younger. Now I know you've been to Christian counseling and all that, but just in case you weren't fixed, you might unwittingly transfer some of the trauma that you experienced as a child onto a child of your own. I do understand your desire to nurture, so my advice is to go to the Nashville Humane Society and adopt another dog because you seem to be very good with pets."

Of course, in retrospect I know that poor woman was just a crooked little tree. She'd likely experienced such a furious storm or serious emotional drought that her trunk was tragically bent, limiting her ability to bear good fruit. Which means I should've treated her with the kindness and respect that all God's image bearers deserve, but I shouldn't have heeded the words that fell out of her mouth because they weren't congruent with God's Word. However, my greatest fear in my twenties and thirties and early forties was that the damage in my past had effectively put a lid on my future, likely limiting the possibility of me having my own family. So immediately after our meeting, I put the adoption application I'd printed off and had been praying over at the very back of my file drawer. Then, when I got off work the next afternoon, I drove to an animal shelter and adopted a chocolate lab named Sally with bladder control problems. She was the third dog I'd brought home that season.

It took seven more years before I had enough faith and courage to stick my toe back into the adoption pond. When a friend who runs a crisis pregnancy center asked if I'd be willing to meet a young woman who was a prostitute and hard-core crack addict and who'd gotten pregant by one of her johns, I said yes. It was a miracle that "Marie" (not her real name) chose not to abort her unborn baby, and it felt like another miracle that she chose me to be the adoptive mom. As a result, we did life closely together for the next six months. I went with her to every doctor's appointment, held her hand during ultrasounds, and was the first person after Marie to feel the baby kick. I actually spent Christmas that year with her in a crack house in an effort to help her get clean.

Even though many years have passed since that season, I'm still not at liberty to share the details regarding why, five days before Anna Price was born that March, the adoption fell apart and Marie chose not to enter the residential rehab facility in which we'd arranged for her to start a new life. But I can tell you I felt like someone had stabbed me through the heart with a hot sword. I was devastated by the loss of both Marie and Anna Price, whom the state had unequivically declared to be my daughter. (Marie let me name the baby she was carrying a few months before she was born. I named her Anna after Anna in Luke's Gospel account and Price after my little brother John Price because our family's a tad Jerry Springer-ish, and I felt like that would help redeem our lineage.)

Three weeks later, on April 16th, 2012, my friend Michelle called. She said she knew I was grieving the loss of Anna Price, but she'd just returned home the night before from a trip to Haiti, and while she was there one of the young moms in the village she was visiting died of AIDS, leaving behind a two-and-a-half-year-old daughter named Missy. She explained that since Missy had HIV, tuberculosis, cholera, and was severely malnourished, she needed to be adopted by someone in a First World country who could afford the necessary medical treatment. Otherwise, the doctors in Port-au-Prince said Missy would likely die within a month or two. She said, "Lisa, you're the first person God brought to mind, and I know you're heartbroken right now, but I wonder if you'd still be willing to pray about starting the adoption process with Missy." I replied, "Nope. I've been praying about this for thirty years, Michelle. Go ahead and sign me up."

Two years later, on April 14th, 2014, I brought my little girl, Melissa Price Harper, home from Haiti. She's an eleven-year-old ball of energetic joy now. Her HIV is completely undetectable, and there are no tuberculosis scars on her lungs. Plus, she's gained forty pounds of pure muscle since then, and I've gained thirty-five of a fluffier type of tissue!

If you'd told me in 1981 when I was a seventeen-year-old senior in high school that my vow to adopt would take thirty-three years to fulfill, I'm pretty sure I would've retracted the promise. But now that I'm fifty-seven, and seven years into the redemptive reality of being Missy's mama—nine if you count our adoption journey—I can tell you she was unequivocally worth the wait. When I look back at those decades of delay through the miraculous lens of motherhood, I can now detect the common denominator of God's sovereign mercy in every moment. For me, the end absolutely justified the means. The priceless gift of parenthood proved the lengthy, often arduous journey to it was inherently valuable.

And that's pretty much the overarching theme of the triadic **PARABLE** in Matthew that we're about to explore together: the prize of eternal glory, wherein we will experience the perfect consummation of our relationship with Jesus, will absolutely be worth the wait! Frankly, given the finitude of our oh-so-human minds, we can't begin to comprehend *how much more* joy and peace and contentment will be ours in the future when we're face-to-face with Jesus!

> The verb *chakah* [khaw-kaw'] in Hebrew means "to wait," "to await," "to delay," "to tarry," or "to long for."[1] You'll find this word translated in the following verses: 2 Kings 7:9; Job 32:4; Psalm 33:20; 106:13; Isaiah 8:17; 30:18; and Daniel 12:12. Read some of these passages and describe how "wait" is used in each one.

Read Exodus 32:1-2 and review Psalm 106:13. In light of these passages, would you describe the willingness to wait as being part of God's will? Explain. How has waiting on the Lord been a part of your faith journey?

Review Isaiah 8:17; 30:18 and read Zephaniah 3:17-20. What insight do these verses give you regarding the relationship between waiting and blessing?

The tale of ten bridesmaids in Matthew 25 has multiple interpretive approaches, but the majority of biblical scholars agree that it's an **ESCHATOLOGICAL** story. In other words, the context for this pre-wedding-feast parable is the second coming of Jesus Christ, with the main characters having symbolic referents in the spiritual realm—that is, they're allegorical. Dr. Craig Blomberg—a world-renowned New Testament scholar, member of the second translatory team for the New International Version translation of the Bible, and one of my favorite seminary professors—clarifies that the bridegroom in this story represents King Jesus, our divine bridegroom. He says the ten bridesmaids, maidens, virgins, or girl posse are subordinate characters, with the five wise representing followers of Jesus Christ and the five foolish representing unbelievers. Therefore, the relatively obvious message here at the beginning of Matthew 25 is about attentiveness and readiness with regard to Christ's return.[2]

But there are a few more interesting things from this story to ponder before we jump to application. For instance, conservative commentator Dr. William Hendriksen retitled the parable in his commentary, "The Parable of the Five Foolish and Five Sensible Girls." He noted, like many other scholars, that the terms "virgin" or "bridesmaid" can be misleading since the original Greek word, *parthenos* [par-then'-os], simply referred to Jewish girls who were of marriage-able age. Therefore the young ladies in Jesus' narrative weren't necessarily in the wedding party, they may have simply been friends or even family members of the bride.[3] Dr. Klyne Snodgrass also points out that this is the only parable to begin with the word "then" (or "at that time"), which underscores the context

of the future kingdom.[4] And Dr. James Montgomery Boice makes these three simple yet profound observations about the striking similarities within the seemingly disparate subgroups of wise and foolish chicks: First, all ten were invited to the wedding banquet, which implies all ten had some form of relationship with the betrothed. Second, all ten responded positively to the invitation. Third, all ten fell asleep during the bridegroom's surprisingly long delay.[5]

I'm so glad Jesus painted all ten girls in the less-than-flattering posture of snoring while waiting for the groom. Otherwise, I think it'd be too easy for His disciples—then and now—to sidestep the seriousness of this warning. Their slumbering becomes an especially poignant detail when we remember that this is the third of five parables that make up Jesus' Olivet discourse in Matthew 24–25. In other words, this story was part of an intimate conversation between Jesus and His twelve disciples less than a week before His crucifixion. Mere days before the three men closest to Him—Peter, James, and John— mirrored exactly what most of us would describe as the inappropriate and indifferent behavior depicted by the ten sleeping beauties—they fell asleep in the garden of Gethsemane even after Jesus implored them to stay awake for His sake.

> Read Matthew 26:36-46. Describe a moment or season in your past when, much like Peter, James, and John, you nodded off in your relationship with Jesus.

> Read Galatians 6:9-10 and Matthew 11:28-30. How can we reconcile what may initially seem contradictory in these two biblical directives?

> What type of spiritual caffeine tends to be most effective in reawakening you to the hope of the gospel and your calling as His beloved?

# Learning Redemptive Rhythms

I got a new car a few months ago because my old one was starting to drop important parts like bumpers on the highway. It has a fancy camera right above the speedometer that detects signs of drowsiness, like increased blinking or head nodding. When it catches me starting to doze off, both the steering wheel and the seat vibrate while the perky lady who lives in the dashboard advises me to pull over. It's obvious to her I'm not alert enough to be operating a two-ton vehicle. I can tell you from recent experience that both the buzzing and the bossy lady can be quite disconcerting!

Matthew 25:6 (VOICE) is basically the vibrating, disconcerting moment in this parable:

> And then in the middle of the night, they heard someone call, "The bridegroom is here, finally! Wake up and greet him!"

This announcement is what we down south would call a "holler," because it was loud enough to jolt those sleepyheads awake with the boisterous proclamation that the long-delayed bridegroom was on the horizon and headed their way. At which point, the similarities between the ten women vanish. Five were prepared for his arrival with sufficient oil for their lamps; however, the other five didn't have enough oil to keep their lamps aflame.

Although there's been a lot of debate through the centuries regarding the symbolic significance of the oil, I think Dr. Boice said it best when he advised:

> Don't be sidetracked by trying to work out the meaning of the oil. Some have identified the oil as the Holy Spirit, because the Spirit is sometimes symbolized by oil in Scripture. But if we do that, we will think that a person can have the Holy Spirit and then run out of him, as it were, or that when one runs out he or she needs to get more. The right thing is to forget about the oil entirely and think only about being ready.[6]

The bottom line here isn't about petroleum, it's about spiritual preparedness, especially in the event of a delayed **PAROUSIA**.

Now let's bring the nose of the plane up for a minute. I think a broader view can help delineate the crisis or division that's been established textually between the prepared, wise women and the unprepared, foolish ones. And the most user-friendly contextualization I found comes from Alan Wright's book, *Lover of My Soul*, in which he writes:

> Betrothed couples [in ancient Jewish tradition, as was the context for Matthew 25] could have a lot of fun preparing for marriage. They could share their lives deeply. But there were limits to their intimacy. They belonged to each other, but they didn't wake up daily face to face. Totally committed but not totally united. Plenty to celebrate but still preparing for the real party. Already husband and wife but not yet married. That's the picture of betrothal.[7]

Pastor Wright goes on to describe how, after an ancient Jewish betrothal was legally agreed upon, the bridegroom would go back to his father's house to prepare a place for him and his new wife to live together. He'd often toil for a year—sometimes longer—typically constructing an annex or upper room on the home he grew up in. Or, if he was wealthy, he'd build a brand spanking new house for his bride. However, she didn't get to make runs to Home Depot with her beloved. Tradition compelled her to stay behind with her family, often in a village many miles away. And it wasn't until the groom's dad inspected the finished quarters and officially declared the new room or home to be satisfactory for the young couple to reside in that the bridegroom journeyed back to his beloved's home to retrieve her. When the news of his impending return reached her neighborhood, people lit lanterns and danced in the streets to celebrate.[8]

Can you imagine the devastating sorrow of those five ill-equipped women when it sunk in that they were locked out of the celebration forever? Remember, they presumed relationship with the betrothed. They assumed they'd be welcomed at the party despite the fact that they were unprepared. Surely the saddest people on earth are those who think they have a relationship with God only to realize they are stepping off a cliff that will forever separate them from Him.

Reread Matthew 25:6. What's the loudest spiritual wake-up call you can remember receiving? How did it affect you? Have its jolting effects been long-lasting? Explain.

Read Hebrews 3:12. Regarding this verse, Charles Spurgeon wrote, "If your God is not a living God to you in whom you live and move and have your being, if he does not come into your daily life, but if your religion is a dead and formal thing, then you will soon depart."[9] Where would you place your faith on a scale of 1 (a dead and formal thing) to 10 (in God you live and move and have your being)?

1    2    3    4    5    6    7    8    9    10

Read Ephesians 5:15-16 and Colossians 4:5. How do you think your life would change if you began to live these verses out with intentionality?

In my opinion, one of the most heart-wrenching moments in the **SYNOPTIC GOSPELS** (Matthew, Mark, and Luke, which are the only gospels that include parables) occurs in Matthew 25:11b, when the unprepared bridesmaids cry plaintively to the bridegroom: "Lord, lord, [once again presuming relationship and even lauding the bridegroom with his rightful superlative title] open the door for us!" (NLT). They are desperately hoping that once he realizes it's them he'll open the door. Instead, he replies definitively, "I don't know you" (v. 12), echoing Jesus' earlier warning in Matthew 7:21-23:

> "Not everyone who says to me, 'Lord, Lord,' will enter the kingdom of heaven, but only the one who does the will of my Father in heaven. On that day many will say to me, 'Lord, Lord, didn't we prophesy in your name, drive out demons in your name, and do many miracles in your name?' Then I will announce to them, 'I never knew you. Depart from me, you lawbreakers!'"

Dr. Snodgrass explains that the closed door, the address, "Lord, Lord," and the language of rejection reveal that we are no longer confined to the story world and have moved into the reality in which it portrays. Which he followed with this poetically, poignant observation: "The veil of the parable has become diaphanous, revealing the eschatological judgment it mirrors."[10]

Whether you believe in the preservation of the saints like I do or not, the fact that these women thought they'd be welcomed, but were instead turned away, is sobering. It epitomizes the sorrow of those who assume there will always be more time to engage in a real relationship with Jesus Christ ... until there's not. The spiritual death implied in this story should be a catalyst for gratitude in believers. It's a startlingly blatant reminder that while we were still sinners, God loved us and regenerated our crooked hearts unto salvation!

Perhaps even more importantly, the grief of the women who missed the party should serve to stoke our evangelical coals and prompt us to ask ourselves the question, *Am I doing everything I possibly can to share the living hope of Christ with those who are hopeless?* In light of the *how much more* kind of love God has lavished on us, how much more can we be doing to spread the glorious good news of the gospel to the world around us?

You're likely familiar with the old adage, "Preach the gospel at all times. When necessary, use words," which is often attributed to Francis of Assisi, although his biographers dispute it. While it sounds catchy and philanthropic and imminently worthy of a flowery background on Instagram, it's actually a bunch of baloney and not biblically defensible. When Paul speaks of the preaching about Jesus in 1 Corinthians 1:21, the word he uses in the original Greek text is **KERYGMA**, which means an apostolic proclamation of the gospel. No matter how incompetent or foolish we feel when it comes to talking to other people about what Jesus has done for us, other image bearers deserve an actual conversation.

In *The Weight of Glory*, C. S. Lewis wrote:

> It is a serious thing to live in a society of possible gods and goddesses, to remember that the dullest and most uninteresting person you can talk to may one day be a creature which, if you say it now, you would be strongly tempted to worship, or else a horror and a corruption such as you now meet, if at all, only in a nightmare.[11]

The allegorical nightmare of the five fictional maidens in Matthew 25—much like the nightmares of those swept away by the flood, the man left in the field, the woman left grinding at the mill, and the wicked servant cut into pieces by his master in the preceding chapter—should serve as a wake-up call for modern-day followers of Christ. We can't forget that while their damnation was irreversible, Christ's love for us is unconditional. And while there were no second chances for them, we've been adopted by a heavenly Father who sprints toward prodigals. Surely that alone is enough to motivate us to run toward the lost and tell them how to be found!

Read 2 Peter 3:8-9. How would you describe the relationship between God's compassion and what, from a human perspective, often seems to be a delayed second coming?

Read Exodus 19:9; 24:12-18; and Mark 13:26. How does Jesus' describing Himself as coming "in clouds" in Mark's Gospel relate to the shekinah glory revealed in the Old Testament Book of Exodus?

Remember, Jesus' disciples were of Jewish descent, so they were familiar with Old Testament narrative. They knew God had revealed Himself to their forefathers in the form of a cloud. So even though this passage in Mark initially reads like a dire warning, it actually contains a glorious promise—it's almost as if Jesus was winking and reminding His followers that when He returns, everything will be OK!

In light of the parable in Matthew 25, how can/should biblical fidelity fuel compassion?

Take a moment and think about this parable. Ten bridesmaids all hanging out together, but five are going to miss the party. Consider the people you hang out with—are they all prepared for Jesus' return? Are there some friends, neighbors, or family members who are going to miss the heavenly party that only those who know Jesus will enjoy? How does this parable heighten your urgency to talk with them about salvation in Jesus?

# Following God's Lead

I love to read; I have since I was a little girl. And when I'm not reading the Bible or some required tome from a seminary class syllabus, you'll usually find me reading a biography—I like true stories. But I read a true story about a young man named Chris several years ago that still haunts me. The once-upon-a-time of his story was April 1992, and the setting was five miles outside of Fairbanks, Alaska. Chris (hitchhiking and going by the alias "Alex") was picked up by a sympathetic truckdriver named James Gallien. When Gallien asked Chris where he was headed, the young man explained he was going to Denali National Park, where he planned to live off the land for a few months.

Mr. Gallien was dubious, noticing the hitchhiker wasn't dressed appropriately for the frigid temperatures. And because Chris was only carrying a relatively small backpack, he obviously didn't have enough provisions for a months-long stay in the wilderness. Spring comes late to the backcountry of Alaska, and most of the territory "Alex" was headed to was still covered under several feet of snow. But they had a nice conversation on the drive to Denali. Chris was likeable and earnest, and once he found out that Gallien was an experienced hunter, he peppered him with questions regarding how to catch small game and what berries he could safely eat in the wild. When Gallien offered to drive out of his way to buy "Alex" some basic essentials, the young man politely refused the offer. Then, when they got to the trailhead, Chris asked his "highway host" to take a picture of him grinning with confidence at the beginning of what he obviously thought would be a grand adventure. Before heading off, he tried to assuage Gallien's concern with these confident parting words, "I'm absolutely positive I won't run into anything I can't deal with on my own."[12]

Gallien later told authorities that he simply couldn't talk "Alex" out of venturing into the wilderness alone. He had no idea that winsome and idealistic hitchhiker's name was actually Chris McCandless. That he was from the Northeast, had graduated from college with honors, and was the only son of loving parents who missed him terribly. James Gallien also had no idea that Chris would die by himself in the Alaskan bush sixteen weeks after they said goodbye at that trailhead.

Chris spent those four months living in an ancient blue and white bus. Several years before, hunters had hauled it into the wilderness to serve as a crude base camp. He left behind a journal on that bus in which he had recorded a few seemingly small mistakes that led to his untimely death. He wrote about getting sick after eating some poisonous plants and how his body was weakened as a result. He wrote about how he tried to hike back to civilization, only ten miles away, but how he was turned back by a swollen river. The last words he wrote were written on a note that two hikers found tacked by his door. The note read: "S.O.S. I need your help. I am injured, near death, and too weak to hike out of here. I am all alone, this is no joke. In the name of God, please remain to save me. I am out collecting berries close by and shall return this evening. Thank you, Chris McCandless. August?"[13] He'd been dead for almost three weeks when the hikers found his body huddled in a sleeping bag his mother had sewn him inside that old bus.[14]

My guess is that Mr. Gallien deeply regrets the day he pulled over to pick up Chris McCandless. He's probably suffered from undeserved guilt over not being able to dissuade a headstrong young man from trekking toward his own tragedy. *How much more* it moves the heart of God when His beloved image bearers are traipsing toward doom and eternal separation from Him. Therefore, He doesn't simply give us a polite lecture in the hope of changing our minds; He bellows warnings for us to watch where we're walking when we get too close to the edge of death. He rages at the darkness trying to swallow our souls. And it seems He stretches time itself to increase our chances to choose life eternal.

With that in mind, I invite you once again to find a relatively quiet place where you can be alone for at least ten minutes. Open your Bible to Matthew 25:1-13 and slowly peruse the whole passage. Talk to God about your own salvation experience. Confess when and how you've gotten "sleepy" on your walk of faith and ask for forgiveness. Praise Him for the help He'll give you to become more alert to His Spirit and attuned to His will. Tell Him about the precious people in your life who don't have any oil in their lamps yet and are foolhardy in their assumption that there will always be more time to deal with "spiritual stuff." Ask Him to break your heart over what breaks His, like people who cry, "Lord, Lord," but don't actually have a relationship with Him.

Feel free to use the lines below to journal your prayers and how you sense the Holy Spirit guiding you with regard to developing a more tender heart for people who don't yet have a real relationship with Jesus, as well as more passion to share the living hope of the gospel.

Read 2 Peter 3:8-9 and John 3:16-17, and write a responsive prayer about how God's warnings are rooted in His concern for our well-being. He loves us way too much to watch us turn away from Him and trek toward tragedy.

DEAR GOD, THANK YOU FOR MOVING HEAVEN AND EARTH TO SAVE ME. THESE ARE THE PEOPLE YOU PROMPTED TO SHARE THE STORY AND LOVE OF JESUS CHRIST WITH ME:

THESE ARE THE SPECIFIC EVENTS YOU ORCHESTRATED THAT REVEALED MY NEED FOR SALVATION:

AND NOW THAT I LOOK BACK, THIS IS HOW YOU EFFECTIVELY STRETCHED TIME IN MY LIFE SO AS TO LEAD ME TO YOU:

# Dancing For Good

My mom turned eighty years old recently, so Missy and I surprised her by flying to Florida. And while we had a wonderful time celebrating Mom, I made another visit alone that weekend that was anything but celebratory. I went back to the crack house where I'd spent so much time with Marie in 2011 and 2012.

I desperately hoped she wouldn't be there when I knocked on that familiar dilapidated door. I hoped maybe she'd finally agreed to go to rehab. Maybe she'd gotten clean and gotten a job serving fast food instead of serving up her petite, track-marked body to abusive johns. Unfortunately, that's not what happened. After I pounded on the door for several minutes, it cracked open to reveal her scowling new pimp and his growling pit bull. When I calmly assured him that I was an old friend of Marie's and not an undercover cop, he swung the door all the way open and gestured dismissively toward her with an expletive.

She was sprawled out on the same threadbare couch I remembered and was obviously high because her eyes were unfocused and her head was lolling from side to side. I softly told her who I was and that I still loved her. She mumbled she didn't remember me and was waiting for a "boyfriend"—which meant her pimp was about to hand her over to some stranger to do whatever he wanted with her in exchange for $15 or $20. Then she asked groggily if I could loan her a few bucks because she really needed another hit. I left another piece of my heart with that precious girl in that dreadful shack and cried the whole way back to my mother's house.

When I got there—red-eyed and disheveled since I'd been crying so hard— I explained where I'd been to Mom and my Aunt Darlene, who was visiting. Darlene exclaimed, "Oh, Lisa, why did you put yourself through the agony of going back there?" I choked back the reply, "I had to, Darlene, I just had to. Because I still hope that one day I'll knock on that door and Marie won't be there anymore."

I don't think disappointment or even anguish when our journey seems especially long is what distances us from God. I believe apathy does. In the tiny margin above Matthew 25 in my Bible, I've written 2 Peter 3:8-9 and Ecclesiastes 3:11. These references help me remember that a thousand years is like one day with God, so He's not slow in keeping His promises as we understand slowness. Plus,

He's planted the mystery of eternity in the human heart, which means we'll always long for what we won't be able to truly experience until we get to our real home in heaven. Next to those references I've written, "Look Up and Lean In" to remind myself to stay hopefully expectant even when it feels like I'm running on fumes.

Because the wedding feast of the Lamb will absolutely be worth the wait.

Because every hard season and uphill step in our lives will make sense when viewed through the lens of eternity.

Because grieving in the already proves you still have faith for the not yet.

To me, the resounding takeaway from the parable of the ten bridesmaids is this: Don't lose sight of the prize when the process gets hard, because He *is* coming back for us. May we seek to be content in Christ and passionate about sharing Him with the "spiritual sleepers" around us, all the while eagerly awaiting His return.

One of the best dancing for good moves we can make in light of this parable is to become more aware that time is passing, and there will soon come a time when there's no time left for the people we love to meet Jesus. Which brings to mind the words of slain missionary Jim Elliot: "When it comes time to die, make sure that all you have to do is die."[15]

> In his classic book, *Interpreting the Parables*, Dr. Blomberg writes, "Jesus' parables leave no neutral ground for casual interest or idle curiosity. They sharply divided their original audiences into disciples and opponents."[16] How has the parable of the ten bridesmaids plowed up any "neutral ground"—ambivalence or apathy—in your heart regarding personal evangelism and sharing the living hope of the gospel of Jesus Christ?

Read Ecclesiastes 3:11. How does the fact that God has planted the mystery of eternity in your heart strike you? Do you find yourself longing more or less for eternity now than you did when you were younger? Explain.

Read John 3:16-17. Who first comes to mind when you think about a follower of Christ who probably doesn't get the "so" part of God's love yet? How could you help this person become more aware of the largess of His grace?

# Wonderful, Weighty Words

The following theological terms can help you better comprehend and communicate the *how much more* aspect of God's love, or, at the very least, help you impress folks at future dinner parties!

**PARABLE:** "An extended metaphor or simile frequently becoming a brief narrative, generally used in biblical times for didactic purposes"[17]

**SYNOPTIC GOSPELS:** "The term applied to Matthew, Mark, and Luke because they see the ministry of Jesus from generally the same point of view, which is quite different from that of the Gospel of John. The similarities among these three Gospels include their use of a common outline: introduction; ministry of John the Baptist and the baptism and temptation of Jesus; greater Galilean ministry; journey and ministry through Samaria, Perea, and rural Judea; and passion week, death, and resurrection of Jesus in Jerusalem. They also record the same emphasis in the teaching of Jesus—the presence, nature, and implementation of the kingdom of God. Furthermore, these three Gospels relate much of the same material, usually in the same order, and often with similar or identical words."[18]

**KERYGMA [KUH·RIG·MUH]:** Greek word that means the "proclamation" of the gospel of Jesus Christ.[19]

**ESCHATOLOGY:** A theological term that refers to the doctrine of last things, particularly focusing on the second coming of Christ and the events surrounding this event.[20]

**PAROUSIA [PUH·ROO·ZEE·UH]:** "The Greek word parousia used in the New Testament to speak of the arrival (2 Cor 7:6; Phil 1:26) or presence of someone (2 Cor 10:10). It is also used as a technical term to speak of the arrival or presence of Christ in glory at a particular point in the eschatological process (e.g., Matt 24:3). The belief in the Parousia or presence of Christ in glory is firmly rooted in all strands of the NT, though the expectation can be referred to apart from the word (Rev 19:11; 1 Cor 15:23; Mark 13:26; 14:62) or by use of other terms (e.g., apokalypsis in 1 Cor 1:7; 1 Pet 1:7). Even in those books where the person of Christ does not loom large (like the letter of James), the Parousia of the Lord is referred to (James 5:7)."[21]

# How Much More

## MIRACULOUS WHEN GOD CREATES SOMETHING OUT OF NOTHING

In the sixth month, the angel Gabriel was sent by God to
a town in Galilee called Nazareth, to a virgin engaged to
a man named Joseph, of the house of David. The virgin's
name was Mary. And the angel came to her and said,
"Greetings, favored woman! The Lord is with you." But she
was deeply troubled by this statement, wondering what
kind of greeting this could be. Then the angel told her, "Do
not be afraid, Mary, for you have found favor with God.
Now listen: You will conceive and give birth to a son, and
you will name him Jesus. He will be great and will be called
the Son of the Most High, and the Lord God will give him
the throne of his father David. He will reign over the house
of Jacob forever, and his kingdom will have no end."
Mary asked the angel, "How can this be, since I
have not had sexual relations with a man?"
The angel replied to her, "The Holy Spirit will come
upon you, and the power of the Most High will
overshadow you. Therefore, the holy one to be born will
be called the Son of God. And consider your relative
Elizabeth—even she has conceived a son in her old
age, and this is the sixth month for her who was called
childless. For nothing will be impossible with God."

## LUKE 1:26-37

## Session Five: SUGAR AND SPICE AND EVERYTHING NICE

---------------------------------------------------------------

---------------------------------------------------------------

---------------------------------------------------------------

---------------------------------------------------------------

---------------------------------------------------------------

---------------------------------------------------------------

---------------------------------------------------------------

---------------------------------------------------------------

---------------------------------------------------------------

---------------------------------------------------------------

---------------------------------------------------------------

---------------------------------------------------------------

---------------------------------------------------------------

---------------------------------------------------------------

---------------------------------------------------------------

---------------------------------------------------------------

To access the video teaching sessions, use the
instructions in the back of your Bible study book.

## DISCUSSION QUESTIONS

What impacted you the most from the video teaching?

Have you ever been marginalized or made to feel "less than" for being a woman? Explain. How has that affected your willingness to lead?

What do you glean from the fact that Jesus had three women who were very involved in His ministry and among His closest companions?

How do these examples of women in leadership and ministry encourage you in your service for Christ and His church?

How has God equipped you to lead out in kingdom ministry?

What current opportunities do you have to lead out? Is there something holding you back? If so, what is it?

How did this video teaching reveal the redemptive heart and extravagant love of God?

# Stretching Sacred Muscles

Before we go any further, I should go ahead and confess that I've become a bit of a testy traveler. I mean, I absolutely love talking to people about Jesus at churches, conferences, and events around the world, but sometimes I don't like the getting there and coming home part. The planes, trains, hotels, Ubers, and church vans part. I've been an itinerate Bible teacher for the better part of thirty years now, which means I'm on the road almost as often as I'm home in Tennessee. And while I know some people romanticize traveling for a living and assume it's a cushy existence softened by Egyptian cotton sheets, room service, and sparkling bathrooms that someone else cleans, that isn't the sum total of my experience.

On one of my recent trips, my hotel room came with a human-hairs-that-weren't-mine-in-the-bed bonus, along with a cigarette butt surprise in the commode. On the trip prior to that, an elderly and anxious volunteer—who'd never driven to the airport by herself before—was assigned the task of carting me back to the airport when the conference I'd graciously been invited to speak at was over. She got so flustered that she turned on the wrong toll road. Twice. I had to run down the concourse to make my flight. Sprinting through the airport was no big deal when I was in my twenties, thirties, and even forties, but now that I'm in my late fifties, certain body parts that aren't supposed to jostle when I jog, do. It creates quite an awkward experience for both me and anyone who has the misfortune of witnessing my attempt at galloping.

Then there was the time not long ago when Missy and I were flying home to the United States from Israel, and I fell asleep for several hours. Which means I didn't monitor my darling daughter's snack intake over the Atlantic. Suffice it to say, six bags of greasy potato chips were a bit much for her tummy, and it decided to violently propel all of that partially digested junk food up and out of her body. Unfortunately, the timing of Missy's "propulsion" was soon after we landed at O'Hare International Airport in Chicago and were standing in line for customs. Even more unfortunately, the glob that shot out of my gluttonous child landed squarely on the chest of a very, very persnickety businessman in a very, very nice suit!

The bottom line is, I often find myself taking deep breaths to prepare myself before boarding a plane. It's like I'm a long-tailed cat getting ready to enter a room filled with rocking chairs.

Anyway, I was in that already-dreading-the-experience-ahead-of-me mindset a few years ago when I noticed a hyperactive little boy and his obviously exhausted mother heading toward the row I was seated in. In light of his extremely energetic body language and the loud volume of the one-sided conversation he was having with his mom, I instinctively hoped they'd keep walking past me to another row of seats. Alas, no such luck.

By the time they'd gotten situated next to me, I'd learned the little boy's name was Billy, he was six years old, they were traveling to see his grandparents, and this was his very first time flying on an airplane. Pretty soon his attention was captured by what was taking place on the tarmac. He turned and pressed his nose to the glass of the porthole window and began narrating everything to his mom, who was sitting between us. He enthusiastically described the size and shape of every single piece of luggage that was crawling up the conveyer belt into the belly of our aircraft. Then, squealing with excitement when another jet pulled up to the gate next to ours, young William began describing that plane's particulars. His voice increased in both speed and decibels during our taxi and takeoff as he tried to make himself heard over the sound of a 747 leaving the ground. However, once we were in the air, he was curiously silent.

After a moment or two, I glanced over his mother's magazine to make sure he hadn't swallowed a peanut or something, and I was graced by the sight of a gobsmacked child. Billy's eyes were as big as saucers, and his mouth formed a silent "O." When he recovered his voice and resumed his animated commentary, I closed my book, leaned back against the headrest, and really listened to his exultations. My prickliness morphed into patience and my grumpy heart softened with grace when I heard him compare the clouds to cotton candy and the houses below us to ants. After seeing that precious little boy's cherubic face illuminated with wonder, I found myself noticing the beautiful patchwork of scenery below us with fresh eyes and remembered what a miracle it actually is to fly from one place to another in a winged metal tube—something that humankind considered an outlandish impossibility little more than a century ago, before those two brothers named Orville and Wilbur harnessed the wind.

My guess is you've heard the birth narrative from Luke's Gospel account almost as many times as I've flown in an airplane. These verses regarding the birth of Jesus Christ are recognized the world over by Christians and non-Christians alike. Even agnostics with holiday shopping lists get to hear Mariah Carey's voice singing about Luke's biblical proclamation at the mall every November and

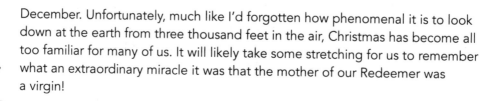

December. Unfortunately, much like I'd forgotten how phenomenal it is to look down at the earth from three thousand feet in the air, Christmas has become all too familiar for many of us. It will likely take some stretching for us to remember what an extraordinary miracle it was that the mother of our Redeemer was a virgin!

The Greek word *thaumazō* [thou-mad'-zo]—which means to "be amazed" or to "be astonished"—appears in the New Testament more than forty times, including Matthew 15:31; Luke 11:14; and Acts 2:7.[1] Read these three verses, then record something God has done recently in your life or your church that amazed you.

Read Mark 6:45-52. When have you been "completely astounded" (v. 51) by how Jesus quieted a storm in your personal life? Since Mark describes the disciples as being hard-hearted (v. 52) right after they were astounded, do you think being astounded by Jesus can sometimes actually be attributed to a lack of faith that He can do the impossible? Why or why not?

Read Luke 2:15-20. How would you describe the difference between the wonder people experienced when the shepherds told them about finding baby Jesus lying in a manger and the way Mary pondered the events surrounding His birth?

Mind you, the Bible isn't the only ancient literature that includes some type of virgin birth story. Greek mythology has several scintillating tales about human women becoming pregnant sans sexual intercourse with a man, then giving birth. However, in each of these fantastical legends the human mamas got frisky with one of the gods in the **PANTHEON**, which resulted in half god/half human offspring. This was the case with the fictional births of Perseus and Hercules.

The difference between Jesus' birth and these pagan fables is huge. The most notable disparity is the lack of sexual intercourse in the biblical narrative. The lustful leer of Zeus—whom Greek mythology describes as a known philanderer and rapist who had dozens of affairs, mistresses, and illegitimate children through the ages—stands in stark contrast to the gentle—even gentlemanly—way the angel Gabriel greeted Mary and gave her a peek at her spiritual sonogram:

> Gabriel appeared to her and said, "Greetings, favored woman! The Lord is with you!"
> Confused and disturbed, Mary tried to think what the angel could mean. "Don't be afraid, Mary," the angel told her, "for you have found favor with God! You will conceive and give birth to a son, and you will name him Jesus. He will be very great and will be called the Son of the Most High. The Lord God will give him the throne of his ancestor David. And he will reign over Israel forever; his Kingdom will never end!"
> Mary asked the angel, "But how can this happen? I am a virgin."
> The angel replied, "The Holy Spirit will come upon you, and the power of the Most High will overshadow you. So the baby to be born will be holy, and he will be called the Son of God."

**LUKE 1:28-35, NLT**

And to make this oh-so-important point about the chaste—albeit powerful—genesis of Mary's pregnancy even clearer, the original Greek word Luke used to describe how the Holy Spirit would "come upon" her in verse 35 is *eperchomai* [ep-er'-khom-ahee], which also means "to draw near." The same word is used again at the beginning of Acts, when, right before Jesus ascended into heaven to sit at the right hand of God the Father, He promised His followers that the Holy Spirit was coming.[2]

While he was with them, he commanded them not to leave Jerusalem, but to wait for the Father's promise. "Which," he said, "you have heard me speak about; for John baptized with water, but you will be baptized with the Holy Spirit in a few days." So when they had come together, they asked him, "Lord, are you restoring the kingdom to Israel at this time?" He said to them, "It is not for you to know times or periods that the Father has set by his own authority. But you will receive power *when the Holy Spirit has come on you*, and you will be my witnesses in Jerusalem, in all Judea and Samaria, and to the ends of the earth."

## ACTS 1:4-8, EMPHASIS MINE

The evangelistic quickening that happened after the Holy Spirit came upon those early disciples underscores the fact that when the Holy Spirit came upon Mary, it wasn't carnal or lascivious in nature. The young woman God chose to carry the incarnation didn't have sex with a man, much less the Holy Spirit. Her pregnancy wasn't biological; our Creator Redeemer brought something out of nothing. Vibrancy from void. *How much more* miraculous could Christmas be!

Read Isaiah 7:14 and Matthew 1:22-23. What facet of how Jesus' birth fulfilled Isaiah's prophecy encourages you the most?

Read Luke 1:46-55,68-79. What are the similarities and the differences between these two celebratory "birth" songs—the first, from Mary, a soon-to-be young mama, and the second, from Zechariah, a had-just-become old daddy?

When the Holy Spirit came upon the disciples in Acts, they were empowered to effectively proclaim the gospel—the good news of Jesus Christ. Does Christmas typically boost your commitment to share the story of Immanuel, God with us? If so, how? If not, why not?

# Learning Redemptive Rhythms

Although the Holy Spirit's New Testament debutant party in Acts isn't quite as familiar as Luke's Christmas story—and not nearly as nostalgic as Advent plays where children dress up in bathrobes and pretend to be shepherds—it was still something to write home about:

> When the day of Pentecost had arrived, they were all together in one place. Suddenly a sound like that of a violent rushing wind came from heaven, and it filled the whole house where they were staying. They saw tongues like flames of fire that separated and rested on each one of them. Then they were all filled with the Holy Spirit and began to speak in different tongues, as the Spirit enabled them. Now there were Jews staying in Jerusalem, devout people from every nation under heaven. When this sound occurred, a crowd came together and was confused because each one heard them speaking in his own language. They were astounded and amazed, saying, "Look, aren't all these who are speaking Galileans? How is it that each of us can hear them in our own native language? Parthians, Medes, Elamites; those who live in Mesopotamia, in Judea and Cappadocia, Pontus and Asia, Phrygia and Pamphylia, Egypt and the parts of Libya near Cyrene; visitors from Rome (both Jews and converts), Cretans and Arabs—we hear them declaring the magnificent acts of God in our own tongues." They were all astounded and perplexed, saying to one another, "What does this mean?" But some sneered and said, "They're drunk on new wine."

**ACTS 2:1-13**

There was no feeding trough birth or sky filled with angels, but Doctor Luke described the Holy Spirit's arrival with just as much wow factor as Christmas. (Luke wrote the Book of Acts immediately after penning his gospel account; in fact, some theologians assert that Luke-Acts was originally one narrative.) Can't you just imagine the stupefied expressions framed by windblown coiffures of that ancient audience who witnessed these divine pyrotechnics? Plus, the backdrop of Pentecost means there were lots of stunned partygoers at this wind-and-fire soiree.

Pentecost—or the Feast of Weeks—was a massive celebration. Adults got paid vacation days, kids got out of school, and grandmothers baked for weeks prior to the big event. People from all over the civilized world (Luke lists both Jews and Gentiles from at least fifteen nations in attendance) made the pilgrimage to Jerusalem to celebrate. Not unlike the World Cup. Or the Super Bowl. Or Mardi Gras. Or the semiannual shoe sale at Nordstrom.

The ethnic and language barriers that likely existed at the beginning of this international gathering quickly dissipated when the disciples were filled with the power of the Holy Spirit and spoke in tongues. And in this particular situation, it wasn't the kind of ecstatic speech that's often associated with biblical tongues, but *known* languages (Acts 2:6,8). That means all these different people groups, from at least fifteen different countries, who spoke completely different dialects (if not completely different languages) heard about the unconditional, redemptive love of Jesus Christ in their native tongue!

> Read John 14:12-17; 15:26-27; and 16:7-8. The Greek term translated to mean Holy Spirit in these passages is *parakletōs* [par-ak-lay-tos], which literally means "called to one's side."[3] However, *parakletōs* is translated into several different terms in our English Bibles, including: "Helper" (ESV, NASB), "Counselor" (CSB), "Advocate" (NIV), and "Comforter" (KJV). Which of those four terms would you say best describes your relationship with the Holy Spirit? In what ways has the Holy Spirit been all four of these in your life?

> Read Romans 8:12-17. Even though the "Spirit of adoption" or "Spirit of sonship" (BSB) is only used this one time in Scripture to describe the Holy Spirit (v. 15), ancient church father John Calvin insisted that it should be His title![4] How has the Holy Spirit—or Spirit of sonship/adoption—reminded you lately that you have the right to call the Creator of the universe "Dad"?

Read Genesis 1:2,26-27; Numbers 11:26-27; Psalm 51:10-11; 139:7-12; and Isaiah 63:10-11. Although scriptural evidence makes it clear that the Holy Spirit is an equal part of our triune God (along with God the Father and God the Son) and has obviously been very active in redemptive history since Creation, why do you think many modern-day followers of Christ tend to associate Him mostly with the supernatural—and often doctrinally controversial—facets of Acts 2?

Can you imagine being in a foreign country where you couldn't understand a word people were speaking around you when, suddenly, in a flash, you were able to speak and understand everything fluently?

My friend Megan can. I met Megan in 2012—the day after I met Missy—in a small town called Gressier, not far from where my daughter was born. Megan moved there in her early twenties soon after she graduated from college, because that's what she sensed God prompting her to do. Even though she had only been a follower of Christ for a short time, she was already radically obedient. Some might even call her crazy obedient. Megan had moved to Haiti not knowing where she was going to live or what exactly God was calling her to do. And she didn't speak a word of Creole.

She said the first few months were really difficult. She'd had every creature comfort in the States but was now living in a hut without running water or electricity. She'd been surrounded by friends in college but was now alone. She'd graduated with honors but was now having a hard time forming simple sentences in the native language. But one constant she hadn't left behind was communicating with the Father. So almost every day she hiked up the highest hill in Gressier to pray. On one prayer trek—a few months after she'd moved to Haiti—Megan came across two little girls who were in obvious distress because they were Restaveks (child slaves) who'd been mistreated by their owner.

Megan stopped to try and assist them, which breached their dam of despair and released a torrent of words she couldn't understand. She was deeply frustrated at that point, knowing God had brought her to Haiti to help people, but the fact that she couldn't speak or understand Creole left her being the one who felt helpless. So she prayed an audacious prayer right then and there, asking God to

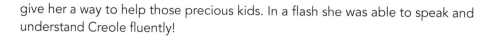

give her a way to help those precious kids. In a flash she was able to speak and understand Creole fluently!

We were hiking up that very same hill—toward several buildings bustling with joyful activity that make up the school, community center, and hospital that Megan Boudreaux Anderson and her husband Josh have since built through their ministry, Respire Haiti—when she shared that story. No drama. No spotlight. Not even an iPhone to capture a compelling social media post. Just two chicks trudging up a steep dirt trail in oppressive heat when I said, "I'm trying to learn Creole so I can communicate with Missy, but I'm having a hard time picking it up. How long did it take you to learn?" Tears were mingling with the perspiration running down my face by the time she finished explaining how she'd "learned" to speak Creole. I couldn't help asking, "Megan, do you realize you experienced a modern-day Pentecost?" She replied with quiet humility, "Yeah, I guess I did." (The rest of Megan's miraculous encounter and many others are in her book, *Miracle on Voodoo Mountain*.)

The disciples in Acts and Megan in Haiti all represent followers of Christ who were desperate to share His love with the broken world around them but utterly unable to communicate the gospel in a way that it could be understood. That is, until the Holy Spirit came upon them and gave them what they couldn't possibly generate by themselves. Comprehension in the midst of confusion. Healing in the midst of hurt. Authority in the midst of anarchy. Something absolutely holy in the midst of nothing but human.

*How much more* miraculous is a God who doesn't take things and situations and people that are already filled with potential and just activate the potential, but instead brings living hope from a complete lack thereof!

Read 1 Peter 3:15. Have there been moments when, like the disciples in Acts 2 and Megan in Haiti, you experienced a legitimate communication barrier when it came to communicating the gospel to someone else? Did you overcome the barrier? If so, how?

The word **PNEUMATOLOGY** refers to theology of the Holy Spirit. How does the virgin birth figure into your pneumatology?

Read Ephesians 1:15-18. What was Paul's goal when he prayed for God to give believers more of His Spirit?

Sit with Acts 2 for a few minutes. Think about the sights, the sounds, the atmosphere of that moment—what it must have been like when the Spirit came down. Now think about this: if you know Christ, that same Holy Spirit lives in you. He wants to work powerfully in and through your life. Are you allowing Him to? What's stopping Him?

# Following God's Lead

Of course, Christmas and Pentecost aren't the only times God made something supernatural out of nothing special. Biblical narrative begins with Him voicing our entire universe into existence from void. Or as my dear friend Christine Caine likes to say with a playful wink, "God sneezed and out came the world."

In the beginning God created the heavens and the earth. Now the earth was formless and empty, darkness covered the surface of the watery depths, and the Spirit of God was hovering over the surface of the waters. *Then God said,* "Let there be light," and there was light. God saw that the light was good, and God separated the light from the darkness. God called the light "day," and the darkness he called "night." There was an evening, and there was a morning: one day. *Then God said,* "Let there be an expanse between the waters, separating water from water." So God made the expanse and separated the water under the expanse from the water above the expanse. And it was so. God called the expanse "sky." Evening came and then morning: the second day.

*Then God said,* "Let the water under the sky be gathered into one place, and let the dry land appear." And it was so. God called the dry land "earth," and the gathering of the water he called "seas." And God saw that it was good. *Then God said,* "Let the earth produce vegetation: seed-bearing plants and fruit trees on the earth bearing fruit with seed in it according to their kinds." And it was so. The earth produced vegetation: seed-bearing plants according to their kinds and trees bearing fruit with seed in it according to their kinds. And God saw that it was good. Evening came and then morning: the third day.

*Then God said,* "Let there be lights in the expanse of the sky to separate the day from the night. They will serve as signs for seasons and for days and years. They will be lights in the expanse of the sky to provide light on the earth." And it was so. God made the two great lights—the greater light to rule over the day and the lesser light to rule over the night—as well as the stars. God placed them in the expanse of the sky to provide light on the earth, to rule the day and the night, and to separate light from darkness. And God saw that it was good. Evening came and then morning: the fourth day.

*Then God said*, "Let the water swarm with living creatures, and let birds fly above the earth across the expanse of the sky." So God created the large sea-creatures and every living creature that moves and swarms in the water, according to their kinds. He also created every winged creature according to its kind. And God saw that it was good. God blessed them: "Be fruitful, multiply, and fill the waters of the seas, and let the birds multiply on the earth." Evening came and then morning: the fifth day.
*Then God said*, "Let the earth produce living creatures according to their kinds: livestock, creatures that crawl, and the wildlife of the earth according to their kinds." And it was so. So God made the wildlife of the earth according to their kinds, the livestock according to their kinds, and all the creatures that crawl on the ground according to their kinds. And God saw that it was good.

*Then God said*, "Let us make man in our image, according to our likeness. They will rule the fish of the sea, the birds of the sky, the livestock, the whole earth, and the creatures that crawl on the earth."

So God created man in his own image; he created him in the image of God; he created them male and female.

God blessed them, and God said to them, "Be fruitful, multiply, fill the earth, and subdue it. Rule the fish of the sea, the birds of the sky, and every creature that crawls on the earth." God also said, "Look, I have given you every seed-bearing plant on the surface of the entire earth and every tree whose fruit contains seed. This will be food for you, for all the wildlife of the earth, for every bird of the sky, and for every creature that crawls on the earth—everything having the breath of life in it—I have given every green plant for food."And it was so. God saw all that he had made, and it was very good indeed. Evening came and then morning: the sixth day.

**GENESIS 1:1-31, EMPHASIS MINE**

A few chapters later, God's voice resounds in the ears, minds, and hearts of an infertile, octogenarian couple, after which they head on over to Costco to stock up on Pampers. Then after a few soap-opera worthy twists and turns in Abe and Sarah's story, a theocracy is born.

*The LORD said to Abram*: Go from your land, your relatives,
and your father's house to the land that I will show
you. I will make you into a great nation,
I will bless you, I will make your name great,
and you will be a blessing. I will bless those who bless you,
I will curse anyone who treats you with contempt, and all
the peoples on earth will be blessed through you.

### GENESIS 12:1-3, EMPHASIS MINE

After these events, *the word of the LORD came to
Abram* in a vision: Do not be afraid, Abram.
I am your shield; your reward will be very great.
But Abram said, "Lord GOD, what can you give me, since
I am childless and the heir of my house is Eliezer of
Damascus?" Abram continued, "Look, you have given me
no offspring, so a slave born in my house will be my heir."
*Now the word of the LORD came to him:* "This one will not be
your heir; instead, one who comes from your own body will
be your heir." *He took him outside and said,* "Look at the
sky and count the stars, if you are able to count them." *Then
he said to him,* "Your offspring will be that numerous."

### GENESIS 15:1-5, EMPHASIS MINE

*The LORD came to Sarah as he had said, and the LORD did for
Sarah what he had promised.* Sarah became pregnant and bore
a son to Abraham in his old age, at the appointed time God had
told him. Abraham named his son who was born to him—the one
Sarah bore to him—Isaac. When his son Isaac was eight days old,
Abraham circumcised him, as God had commanded him. Abraham
was a hundred years old when his son Isaac was born to him.

### GENESIS 21:1-5, EMPHASIS MINE

A few miles down the road of redemptive history, when the prophet Ezekiel was standing on a cliff lamenting the valley of dry bones below, God's booming voice entered biblical narrative yet again. The result: that graveyard transformed into a sanctuary filled with living, breathing worshipers:

> The hand of the LORD was on me, and he brought me out by his Spirit and set me down in the middle of the valley; it was full of bones. He led me all around them. There were a great many of them on the surface of the valley, and they were very dry. Then he said to me, "Son of man, can these bones live?" I replied, "Lord GOD, only you know."
>
> *He said to me,* "Prophesy concerning these bones and say to them: Dry bones, hear the word of the LORD! *This is what the LORD God says to these bones:* I will cause breath to enter you, and you will live. I will put tendons on you, make flesh grow on you, and cover you with skin. I will put breath in you so that you come to life. Then you will know that I am the LORD."
>
> So I prophesied as I had been commanded. While I was prophesying, there was a noise, a rattling sound, and the bones came together, bone to bone. As I looked, tendons appeared on them, flesh grew, and skin covered them, but there was no breath in them. *He said to me,* "Prophesy to the breath, prophesy, son of man. Say to it: *This is what the Lord GOD says:* Breath, come from the four winds and breathe into these slain so that they may live!" So I prophesied as he commanded me; the breath entered them, and they came to life and stood on their feet, a vast army. *Then he said to me,* "Son of man, these bones are the whole house of Israel. Look how they say, 'Our bones are dried up, and our hope has perished; we are cut off.' Therefore, prophesy and say to them, '*This is what the Lord GOD says: I am going to open your graves and bring you up from them, my people, and lead you into the land of Israel. You will know that I am the LORD, my people, when I open your graves and bring you up from them. I will put my Spirit in you, and you will live,* and I will settle you in your own land. Then you will know that I am the LORD. I have spoken, and I will do it. *This is the declaration of the LORD.'*"

### EZEKIEL 37:1-14, EMPHASIS MINE

Therefore, it really shouldn't surprise us when we turn the pages of Scripture to discover the redemptive potency of His Spirit at Christmas and in establishing the early church in the Book of Acts. God had already revealed His plan wasn't to make good things better but to make something miraculous out of nothing special—pure light out of pitch black, **IMAGO DEI** out of dust, Israelites out of infertility, sanctuaries out of cemeteries! And my favorite death-to-life biblical revelation is that the Spirit of God actually brought the Son of God back to life:

> Now if Christ is in you, the body is dead because of sin, but the Spirit gives life because of righteousness. And if *the Spirit of him who raised Jesus from the dead* lives in you, then he who raised Christ from the dead will also bring your mortal bodies to life through his Spirit who lives in you.

### ROMANS 8:10-1, EMPHASIS MINE

> For Christ also suffered for sins once for all, the righteous for the unrighteous, that he might bring you to God. *He was put to death in the flesh but made alive by the Spirit.*

### 1 PETER 3:18, EMPHASIS MINE

Jesus didn't resuscitate Himself, y'all. The Spirit of God resurrected Him from the dead. Which translates into a radically more abundant life than most of us would dare to pray for. It means when you feel like you're at the very end of your rope, like you don't have one drop left in your emotional gas tank, like there's absolutely no way you can keep hiking up the heartbreaking hill you've been climbing, like you're just bone-tired ... well then, you're at the exact point of hopelessness where the Holy Spirit always gives mouth-to-mouth resuscitation. He can breathe divine life back into collapsed lungs! And *how much more* our Creator Redeemer loves us—His children—than a huge pile of skeletons!

With that in mind, I invite you to again find a relatively quiet place where you can be alone for at least ten minutes. Then open your Bible and reread Luke 1:26-37 and Acts 2:1-13. Talk to God about the areas of your life that feel barren and weak. Tell Him where you desperately need His Spirit to come upon you and bring life and strength. Confess when and how you've forgotten the miracles of Christmas and Pentecost and all of the other moments in biblical history where He made something supernatural out of nothing special. Ask God

to speak to your heart and stir up your faith just as He did with Mary and the disciples in Acts.

Feel free to use the lines below to journal your prayers and how you sense the Holy Spirit drawing close to you and increasing your capacity to believe that God will do the impossible and create something supernatural out of the nothing-specials in your life.

Now read Ezekiel 37:1-14 and write a responsive prayer below, asking God to stir your faith enough to believe in resurrection-power miracles regarding the desires, dreams, and relationships that have died along the way in your own story.

> GOD grabbed me. GOD's Spirit took me up and set me down in the middle of an open plain strewn with bones. He led me around and among them—a lot of bones! There were bones all over the plain—dry bones, bleached by the sun.

**EZEKIEL 37:1-2, MSG**

Confess what looks/feels like dry bones in your own life—the unfulfilled desires, unrealized dreams, and broken relationships.

He said to me, "Son of man, can these bones live?"
I said, "Master God, only you know that."
He said to me, "Prophesy over these bones:
'Dry bones, listen to the Message of God!'"

**EZEKIEL 37:3-4, MSG**

Ask God for wisdom regarding what seemingly dead desires, dreams, and relationships in your story would be for your good and His glory if they came back to life. Only when you feel like you've heard Him speak clearly regarding what should be enlivened, list them below.

Write your own prayer echoing the way that Ezekiel not only believed but acted on God's promise that He would make dry bones live.

# Dancing For Good

We know that God, who raised the Lord Jesus, will also
raise us with Jesus and present us to himself together
with you. All of this is for your benefit. And as God's
grace reaches more and more people, there will be great
thanksgiving, and God will receive more and more glory.
That is why we never give up. Though our bodies are dying, our
spirits are being renewed every day. For our present troubles are
small and won't last very long. Yet they produce for us a glory
that vastly outweighs them and will last forever! So we don't
look at the troubles we can see now; rather, we fix our gaze
on things that cannot be seen. For the things we see now will
soon be gone, but the things we cannot see will last forever.

**2 CORINTHIANS 4:14-18, NLT**

My brother-in-law James passed away tragically and unexpectedly in the
spring of 2020. This was only a month after COVID-19 was declared a global
pandemic, a time when it seemed the entire planet was already grappling with
some measure of grief and anxiety. I remember all too well those very long, hard,
heartbreaking days that followed his untimely death. Of course, his loss is still
acute for all of us who knew and loved him, but the initial impact was brutal.
Every morning I'd wake up to the immediate, terrible memory of his death. The
sorrow was relentless, like being hit by a wave every time you broke the surface
of the ocean in desperate need of a breath of air. I couldn't imagine what my
sister and nephews were going through in the wake of his loss. The fact that
I couldn't do very much—besides listen—to lessen their devastation in the
aftermath of losing James compounded my sadness.

It was in one of those very low moments that my dear friend Allison Allen
dropped by. I was sitting in a rocking chair on our front porch when I saw her
car coming up the driveway. I hurriedly tried to stem the tide of tears that came
often in those early days after James died, but of course my face was still wet
and etched with sadness when she ambled up the front walk. She didn't stay
long, and she didn't say much. Mostly she just sat quietly in the rocking chair
next to me and gave me the gift of presence. But before she left, she handed
me a small brown paper bag full of unmarked bulbs for my garden and gently
encouraged me to plant them when I had the time and energy.

I opened the bag a few days or so later and found the condolence card she'd tucked inside. In Allison's lovely, slanted script, it read: "Just as surely as God will coax flowers to bloom from these dry, brown bulbs, He will bring renewed hope and joy to you and your family from this present sorrow." The note went on to say that she wasn't sure if the bulbs would bloom this year—since the coldest days of winter had already passed—or the following, but when they did she hoped I'd be reminded that God can bring beauty out of barrenness.

Although my heart didn't resonate with the inscribed promise of her note, I went outside and planted those little shriveled up orbs—most of them not any bigger than a peach pit—in the still cold soil of the garden in our front yard. I'd all but forgotten about them until one hot and humid morning in the middle of July, about three and a half months after James died. I was standing at the kitchen sink looking out our front window and was startled by a huge yellow bloom the size of a dinner plate. I hustled outside to find myself staring at an extremely large and luminous dahlia.

I've been a gardening enthusiast my entire adult life and have planted blooming perennials of almost every size and shape and color. But for some reason I've never grown dahlias. Named after a Swedish botanist, Anders Dahl, in the late 1700s, dahlias are known for their vibrancy and the size of their blooms, which can measure as wide as fifteen inches.[5] The bulbs Allison had given me were one of the "giant" varieties and had sprouted to almost four feet tall, seemingly overnight, with gorgeous blooms bigger than my head!

Peering into the face of that unexpected flower, I sensed a quiet pulse of hope in my heavy heart. I began to walk around our hilltop property with fresh eyes that day and couldn't help noticing how the peach trees I'd planted only a few years ago (to camouflage the big, ugly, pokey-outy green top of a submerged propane tank) were now laden with hundreds, maybe thousands, of peaches. The smell was heavenly. Little apples had sprouted from the white flowers that covered our apple trees only a few weeks before, and red plums looked like they were playing hide-and-seek throughout our mini orchard, peeking out from behind almost every leaf. Tomatoes and blackberries and blueberries and strawberries and herbs all seemed to be shouting happily for attention, "Hey, y'all! Look at how big we're getting!" And the irises and roses and lavender and jasmine swayed in the breeze like a collaborative dance troupe. I found myself smiling, in spite of my ache, as I remembered the miracle nature performs every year when the austere barrenness of winter gives way to the abundant and

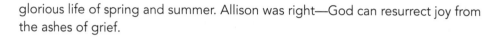

glorious life of spring and summer. Allison was right—God can resurrect joy from the ashes of grief.

Yes, we live in a broken world that is marred by gut-wrenching loss, great pain, and global pandemics, but God's compassionate presence is never absent, no matter how bleak and barren the season. There's always reason for hope, because time and time again His Spirit has brought life where there seemed to be nothing but death.

One of the best dancing for good moves we can make in light of the plethora of biblical examples of how God brings beauty out of barrenness is to hang on to hope. Because the Holy Spirit raised Jesus back to life from death on that first Resurrection Sunday over two thousand years ago, death no longer has the final say. Life does. Therefore, we really don't have to grieve as those who have no hope. We can choose hope and speak life and love, even when it's hard.

> Read John 12:24-26. How have you experienced unexpected life from what you initially feared was your most painful loss?

> Read Psalm 30:11-12. Would you describe the season you're currently in as more of a mourning or a dancing time? How does God's presence and comfort during past seasons of mourning inform your future?

> Read 1 Corinthians 1:26-31. What's your favorite "what is viewed as nothing" (v. 28) facet of your own life that God has used to bring Himself glory? What supernatural miracle are you currently praying God will bring out of nothing special?

# Wonderful, Weighty Words

The following theological terms can help you better comprehend and communicate the *how much more* aspect of God's love, or, at the very least, help you impress folks at future dinner parties!

**PANTHEON:** "The gods of a particular mythology considered collectively."[6]

**GRECO-ROMAN POLYTHEISM:** "A complex interplay of not only the pantheons of Greece and Rome, but also the many foreign gods and goddesses of other cultures, such as Egypt, Israel and the many indigenous groups of Asia Minor."[7]

**PNEUMATOLOGY:** The study of the Holy Spirit's person and work. The term is derived from the Greek *pneuma* (spirit).[8]

**VIRGINAL CONCEPTION OF JESUS:** "The belief that Jesus was conceived by the Virgin Mary by the power of the Holy Spirit without a human father involved in conception (Matt. 1; Luke 1–2). The term is often used synonymously with the 'virgin birth of Jesus.'"[9]

## Extra Credit Pentecost Information for Inquiring Minds:

"Both the Hebrew Old Testament word for 'spirit'—*ruach*—and the Greek New Testament word for 'spirit'—*pneuma*—are onomatopoeic terms. Which means the sound made when saying the word actually conveys its basic definition, in this case the expulsion of wind or air in motion."[10] This is much like the way a cartoonist would doodle the word "whack!" above a boxer's punch landing on his opponent's jaw. Thus, the biblical words used for Holy Spirit express in the most fundamental way that He is the breath of life!

Pentecost is the New Testament title for the "Festival of Weeks" or *Shavuot*, which is the Hebrew word for "weeks" in light of the ceremonial law in Leviticus 23:16 instructing the Israelites to count off seven weeks from the end of Passover (when the first bundle of grain reaped from the harvest is presented to the priest) to the day after the seventh Sabbath. That specified time period of seven weeks is also where the English word "Pentecost" came from, because it's a transliteration of the Greek word *pentekostos*, meaning "fifty."[11]

# How Much More

## IS HUMILITY AND SACRIFICE THE WAY OF CHRIST

Before the Passover Festival, Jesus knew that his hour had
come to depart from this world to the Father. Having loved his
own who were in the world, he loved them to the end.
Now when it was time for supper, the devil had already put it into the heart
of Judas, Simon Iscariot's son, to betray him. Jesus knew that the Father
had given everything into his hands, that he had come from God, and
that he was going back to God. So he got up from supper, laid aside his
outer clothing, took a towel, and tied it around himself. Next, he poured
water into a basin and began to wash his disciples' feet and to dry them
with the towel tied around him. He came to Simon Peter, who asked
him, "Lord, are you going to wash my feet?" Jesus answered him, "What
I'm doing you don't realize now, but afterward you will understand."
"You will never wash my feet," Peter said.
Jesus replied, "If I don't wash you, you have no part with me."
Simon Peter said to him, "Lord, not only my feet, but also my hands and my head."
"One who has bathed," Jesus told him, "doesn't need to wash anything except
his feet, but he is completely clean. You are clean, but not all of you." For he
knew who would betray him. This is why he said, "Not all of you are clean."
When Jesus had washed their feet and put on his outer clothing, he reclined
again and said to them, "Do you know what I have done for you? You call
me Teacher and Lord—and you are speaking rightly, since that is what I
am. So if I, your Lord and Teacher, have washed your feet, you also ought
to wash one another's feet. For I have given you an example, that you
also should do just as I have done for you. Truly I tell you, a servant is not
greater than his master, and a messenger is not greater than the one who
sent him. If you know these things, you are blessed if you do them."

## JOHN 13:1-17

# Session Six: ALWAYS FOR OUR GOOD AND HIS GLORY

_____

_____

_____

_____

_____

_____

_____

_____

_____

_____

_____

_____

_____

_____

_____

_____

_____

_____

_____

To access the video teaching sessions, use the
instructions in the back of your Bible study book.

## DISCUSSION QUESTIONS

What impacted you the most from the video teaching?

Would you say you're currently standing out in the culture or blending in? Explain.

What seems to hinder you the most in standing out? What are the consequences personally and for the church if we continue to just blend in?

How does standing in the confidence that you are dearly loved by God affect your walk of faith and your ministry for Him?

How can we better open our arms wide for the difficult people in our lives and for those who seem to be walking away from the faith?

Lisa said Jesus is on every single page of Scripture. What does that mean? Why is it important?

How did this video teaching reveal the redemptive heart and extravagant love of God?

# Stretching Sacred Muscles

I've gotten a lot of parenting credit I don't deserve from the uncommonly smooth adoption transition Missy and I experienced. And while I'd like to think she connected with me so quickly because I'm such a good mama, the truth is our relatively fast and deep mother-daughter bond is Fifi's fruit. Fifi is Missy's great aunt. She's the sickly, gentle, huge-hearted saint who took my little girl in when her lovely biological mama was too sick from AIDS to care for her. (Marie, Missy's mom, never knew she had AIDS because, like far too many impoverished people barely surviving in Third World countries, she had never been diagnosed.) Marie was simply too weak to produce milk, much less scrounge for food for her infant. She was too cold to snuggle her daughter at night and provide necessary warmth. So Fifi stepped in to rescue Missy, becoming the main reason my baby girl survived infancy.

Fifi is also the one who doggedly championed me to be Missy's new mama. Although she'd stepped in to care for Missy soon after she was born, Fifi is elderly and suffers with serious health problems herself. She didn't have the capacity to provide long-term care. Missy needed a forever mama, and Fifi helped make that happen. She did so in spite of the fact that I was an American stranger who, if approved to adopt her beloved great-niece, would take her to a land far, far away called Tennessee. A place filled with four-wheel drive trucks and fried food.

The first time I met Fifi, she smiled shyly while placing a scowling two-and-a-half-year-old Missy into my arms. She then said to her firmly in Creole, "This is your white mama." Both Missy and I protested; I wanted to give Missy ample time to warm up to me, and Missy was obviously alarmed by my pale ampleness. But Fifi just smiled again shyly, crossed her arms, and quietly refused to take the indignant toddler back into her embrace. It took a few minutes for Missy to quit trying to wriggle out of my arms, but when she realized she didn't have a choice in the matter, she grudgingly relented to let me feed her beans and rice.

The next day, at Fifi's insistence, Missy allowed me to hold her hand and walk around the village for an hour. The second night I was there, Missy condescended to sit on my lap during a stifling hot worship service after Fifi gave her a very direct you'd-better-mind-me-right-now-young-lady look. With each new baby-step milestone in our budding relationship, Fifi's smile got wider, and she'd nod with approval. When I hugged her fiecely before leaving at the end of that first of many visits, all the while babbling about how grateful I was, she replied simply, "I love you, praise Jesus"—one of the only English phrases she knew.

Over the next two years those five words became our regular conversation. During long, hot, bumpy bus rides together from their village to Port-au-Prince for a doctor's checkup or an appointment with the U.S. Embassy, Fifi would hold my hand the entire two or three hour trip and repeat softly, "I love you, praise Jesus" every so often. When I tried to engage her with my pitiable attempts to speak Creole (I still have several "Introduction to Creole" books in my library and an "easy" English-Creole app on my phone, but much like Frenchy in the musical *Grease*, I proved to be a language school dropout), she'd nod and listen patiently but would inevitably respond with, "I love you, praise Jesus."

Finally, on April 14, 2014, when I hugged Fifi with tears streaming down my face and Missy sleeping in my arms, clutching a manilla folder with Haitian and American documents proving that I was now legally Missy's adoptive mother, Fifi squeezed both of my hands, looked deep into my eyes, and said once again, "I love you, praise Jesus." By then I knew what she really meant by those five words was, "I'm entrusting you to take good care of her. It's breaking my heart to know I'll probably only see her again a few more times before I die, but I know this is what's best for her. Remember that she likes her mangos on the firm side, and she loves to be sung to sleep. Don't let her be lazy in school, or be disrespecful, or eat with her mouth open, or bite her fingernails, or forget how very much I love her. OK, I'm going to kiss her head one last time and try to memorize her face and her precious little girl smell and the shape of her toes before I turn my head. And please know the reason I won't watch you drive away toward the airport isn't because I'm ambivilant. It's so I won't chase the van and beg you not to leave quite yet."

Fifi willingly gave up her claim on my daughter's heart so that my daughter could live, one of the most selfless acts I've ever had the privilege of witnessing. *How much more* is our Savior's willingless to make Himself "less" so that we can experience abundant life!

Has God ever prompted you to sacrificially step back from a relationship with someone you love for their own good? Perhaps it was a dating relationship or a friendship. Or maybe with one of your children as they prepared to leave home and become more independent? If so, how did you respond?

Read Isaiah 53:1-3; Philippians 2:5-8; and Hebrews 1:3-4. How do you reconcile Isaiah's and Paul's less than flattering descriptions of Jesus with the fact that Hebrews describes Him as the radiance of God's glory?

Read Philippians 2:1-4 and Proverbs 4:23. How would you describe the synergy between considering others as more highly than yourself and healthy self-care/guarding your heart?

When we peruse passages like John 13:1-17, where Jesus washed the feet of His disciples, or Philippians 2:1-11, which describes Jesus as taking "the form of a servant" (v. 7), or 2 Corinthians 8:9, which describes Jesus as becoming poor, it's very, very important to note that by making Himself nothing to become a man (Phil. 2:7), Jesus did not in any way forfeit His deity. When our Savior condescended to earth, wrapped in the smooth olive skin of a Jewish baby boy, whose first cradle was a rough-hewn feeding trough, He was still wholly and completely divine. The same God who spoke the universe into being also cried for His mother's milk. Mind-blowing, isn't it? And please don't be embarrassed if you can't quite wrap your head around this biblical truism of the incarnation—of Jesus being fully God and fully man. It has caused lots of head-scratching through the ages.

As a matter of fact, the very first time a large group of Christian leaders convened for what we would now describe as a "national convention" it was to sort out this very issue. A council was convened in the Bithynian city of Nicea by the early church fathers, prompted by contradictory teachings that were circulating around the Roman empire regarding the divinity of Jesus. They gathered together to prayerfully consider these questions: How do these teachings stack up against the whole of what Scripture teaches? And what are the implications regarding our salvation through Christ alone?

Dr. Bruce Shelley, a theologian and historian (who, until his death in 2010, just so happened to be a long-term and dearly loved professor at my alma mater, Denver Seminary), described that oh-so-important gathering in Nicea in vivid detail:

> July 4, 325 was a memorable day. About three hundred Christian bishops and deacons from the eastern half of the Roman Empire had come to Nicea, a little town near the Bosporus Straits flowing between the Black Sea and the Mediterranean.
>
> In the conference hall where they waited was a table. On it lay an open copy of the Gospels. The emperor, Constantine the Great, entered the hall in his imperial, jewel-encrusted, multicolored brocades, but out of respect for the Christian leaders, without his customary train of soldiers. Constantine spoke only briefly. He told the churchmen they had to come to some agreement on the crucial questions dividing them. "Division in the church," he said, "is worse than war."
>
> The bishops and deacons were deeply impressed. After three centuries of periodic persecutions instigated by some Roman emperor, were they actually gathered before one not as enemies but as allies? Some of them carried scars of the imperial lash. One pastor from Egypt was missing an eye; another was crippled in both hands as a result of red-hot irons. But Constantine had dropped the sword of persecution in order to take up the cross. Just before a decisive battle in 312, he had converted to Christianity.
>
> Nicea symbolized a new day for Christianity. The persecuted followers of the Savior dressed in linen had become the respected advisers of emperors robed in purple. The once-despised religion was on its way to becoming the state religion, the spiritual cement of a single society in which public and private life were united under the control of Christian doctrine. If Christianity were to serve as the cement of the Empire, however, it had to hold one faith. So the emperors called for church councils like Nicea, paid the way for bishops to attend, and pressed church leaders for doctrinal unity.[1]

I doubt they had Tex-Mex food trucks and commemorative T-shirts like the last convention I attended, but I'd bet my bottom dollar they had some really spicy debates in Nicea. Namely because of two wildly divergent Greek terms—*homoiousios* [hoh-moi-oo-see-us], which means "of similar substance" and *homoousios* [hoh-moh-oo-see-us], which means "same in substance."[2] These terms were used in the third and fourth centuries by religious leaders to explain the relationship between Jesus the Son and God the Father. One group argued that the Son was of similar, but not identical substance as God the Father, while another, led by ancient church father and theologian Athanasius, argued that the Son derives His substance from the Father and hence shares the very same substance and nature as the Father. Ultimately, God led that Council at Nicea to adopt the doctrine of *homoousios* as the orthodox position.

But of course all that fussing over the divinity of Jesus didn't completely die out. That prompted another council—the Council of Chalcedon—to be convened in AD 451 to debate the validity of the **DOCETICIST** doctrinal position. Docetists believed that Jesus was fully divine, but He only *appeared* to be fully human. One yahoo from this heretical subset of leaders insisted that when Jesus cried at the tomb of Lazarus, they were faux tears—the tears of an actor. Hard not to roll your eyes, isn't it? Wisely, after much discussion and prayer, this second "National Convention of Christian Leaders" decided that no, Jesus hadn't pulled the wool over anyone's eyes by pretending to be human. Their consensus was that Jesus was indeed fully man during His earthly ministry and yet was without sin. That resulted in another Greek term to impress your small group members with: *hypostasis*, which basically means "being" or "person." It's used to explain how in Jesus Christ we have one person in whom two natures—divine and human—are present at the same time.[3] Which makes the fact that after wielding a scepter in glory, Jesus chose to squat down and pick up a towel and wash the nasty feet of those disciples—one of whom He knew had already thrown Him under the bus for a little extra spending money—all the more breathtakingly lovely, doesn't it?

> What **ANTHROPOMORPHIC** terms would you use to describe Jesus to an unbeliever—without using the words "lion" or "lamb"—to convey His combination of approachability and formidability?

Read Matthew 17:1-8. How does John's first experience with a transfigured Jesus compare to his fainting episode in Revelation 1:9-17?

Read Exodus 34:29-30 and Mark 10:13-16. Do you tend to be more drawn to God's glory that was so intense it caused Moses' face to glow, or to God's grace that compelled kids to launch themselves into His lap? Explain.

# Learning Redemptive Rhythms

Several years ago I heard a true story about a kindergarten Sunday School class that I don't think I'll ever forget. It was Palm Sunday and the teacher wanted to help her young students understand the spiritual significance of Easter. So she began with a question to help establish the motif that many of our major holidays center around Jesus:

"Class, can anyone tell us the meaning of Christmas?" At which point, a five-year-old little boy named George raised his hand and answered, "It's when Jesus became incarnate and all the angels sang, and the shepherds worshiped, and the wise men came bearing gifts to acknowledge Him as king." The teacher, pleasantly surprised, replied, "That was an excellent answer, George," thinking, *His parents must be college professors or something.* Then she asked, "And can someone tell me what today, Palm Sunday, represents?" George was the only child with his hand raised, so after a moment's hesitation, she nodded for him to speak again. He cleared his throat with adult-like-gravitas and then proclaimed earnestly: "It's when Jesus entered Jerusalem riding a young colt and all of the people sang 'Hosanna' and laid down palm branches and heralded Him as the Messiah. It was the beginning of the last week of our Savior's life."

The teacher, now duly impressed if not a tad flustered, posed another question from her lesson plan, "Alright dear ones, who can tell us about Good Friday?" Not surprisingly, the rest of the class was by now too intimidated to venture a guess. So with an indulgent smile she nodded at George again, and with the ease of an experienced pastor, he explained, "Well, that's when Jesus was crucified on a cross for our sins and the temple curtain was torn in two and He gave up His spirit to God the Father on humankind's behalf." Of course, she knew better than to pose the final question to anyone but George, so she closed her lesson book, leaned back into her chair with a mostly happy, slightly resigned sigh, and said, "Honey, why don't you go ahead and tell us all about Easter." Which is when that mini Einstein's clay pedestal collapsed, because he gave a much more stereotypical five-year-old response: "That's when Jesus rose from the dead and came out of the tomb! But when He saw His shadow, He went back in for another three weeks."

I think most of us are a lot like George. We've got the gist of the gospel pretty well figured out but could still use some help with some of the finer points! And surely, one of the finest points about Jesus is His other-worldly humility, which was palpable when He chose to massage the dusty and calloused feet of the "dirty dozen" after dinner on that Maundy Thursday, mere hours before His betrayal and arrest in the garden of Gethsemane. In light of *homoousios*—the fact that Jesus is the very same substance and nature as God the Father—He's perfectly omniscient. This means our Lord and Savior knew exactly what lay ahead of Him that Easter weekend. Yet He still chose to stoop and serve.

> Reread Genesis 1:26-27 and John 1:1-18. How would you explain these complex passages regarding the trinitarian nature of God to a child or non-Christian?

> Read Job 21:22; Psalm 139:1-4; and Romans 11:33-34. What's the common denominator in these passages?

> Imitable theological scholar and pastor, J. I. Packer, wisely said, "A God whom we could understand exhaustively, and whose revelation of Himself confronted us with no mysteries whatsoever, would be a God in man's image, and therefore an imaginary God, not the God of the Bible at all."[4] How would you describe the connection between God's inscrutability (He can't be completely understood by the human mind) and the faith of His people? If your mind actually had the capacity to unravel the mystery of who God is, would you want to? Explain.

I'm admittedly old-fashioned about certain things like civility and treating others with respect; that being said, the current "it's my way or the highway" climate of modern culture is quite alarming to me. Never before in my life have I seen so much narcissistic vitriol passed off as "virtue" as I've observed in the past year

or two. All you have to do is scroll through social media for a few minutes and it becomes apparent that humility and sacrifice are not trending. But then, the way of this world has never been the way of Christ, has it? Paul reminds us of this so well in his first letter to the Corinthians:

> The message of the cross is foolish to those who are headed for destruction! But *we who are being saved* know it is the very power of God.

### 1 CORINTHIANS 1:18, NLT, EMPHASIS MINE

Unfortunately, "we who are being saved" are not immune to egocentrism and self-indulgence. Which probably would've been apparent if someone had polled us church members to ascertain how much toilet paper we hoarded in those first few month of COVID-19. It's easy to post online humblebrags about how "love wins," but it's a whole other thing to live a life bent in the radical position of God-oriented and others-oriented service. That's definitely the portrait of destiny Jesus painted for His followers when He paused at the end of that Passover pedicure.

> After washing their feet, he put his robe on and returned to his place at the table. "Do you understand what I just did?" Jesus said. "You've called me your teacher and lord, and you're right, for that's who I am. So if I'm your teacher and lord and have just washed your dirty feet, then you should follow the example that I've set for you and wash one another's dirty feet. Now do for each other what I have just done for you. I speak to you timeless truth: a servant is not superior to his master, and an apostle is never greater than the one who sent him. So now put into practice what I have done for you, and you will experience a life of happiness enriched with untold blessings!"

### JOHN 13:12-17, TPT

In much the same way that Dr. Boice encouraged us not to get sidetracked by the symbolism of the oil in the parable of the bridesmaids in Matthew 25, Dr. D. A. Carson (another brilliant theologian I have a platonic crush on) warns readers not to assume the central theme of this passage is about the rite of foot washing. Instead, the heart of Jesus' command here in John 13 is about humility and helpfulness toward others.[5] In other words, the *how much more* largess of God's love for us can only be expressed in the context of community through humble acts of kindness and service to each other.

The exclamation point in this narrative is that during this period of ancient history the task of footwashing was normally reserved for only the lowliest of servants. There's actually a well-known rabbinical story about how "when Rabbi Ishmael returned home from synagogue one day and his mother wished to wash his feet, he refused on the ground that the task was too demeaning."[6] I think all too often humility is misinterpreted as demeaning or degrading in modern culture as well, don't you?

The Greek word translated as "example" in John 13:15 is *hypodeigma* [hoop-od'-igue-mah], and it can also be translated "pattern."[7] What follower of Christ in your life has a pattern of extended humble kindness toward others?

Read Mark 10:45. How would you distill Jesus' statement about His purpose here into a modern-day mission statement?

Read Matthew 20:1-16,20-28. What behaviors would you have to change in order to passionately align your heart with Jesus' teaching in this passage? What situations do you tend to be "first" in? What would need to change for you to be "last" in those same scenarios?

Before moving on, stop for a moment and picture yourself at that Passover table. Hear Jesus say, "Do you understand what I just did?" (John 13:12, TPT). Well, do you? What is the personal lesson for you? How does what Jesus did for His disciples move you to serve others?

# Following God's Lead

"I give you a new command: Love one another. Just as I have loved you, you are also to love one another. By this everyone will know that you are my disciples, if you love one another."

## JOHN 13:34-35

Love. I know, it sounds pretty simple doesn't it. But when Jesus gave us this new command to love, the historical context was anything but simple. He spoke these memorable words right after washing His disciples' nasty feet and only a few hours before He was betrayed. Following those events came a bogus trial, more betrayal by His closest friends, being beaten with a cat-of-nine-tails, having a rough-hewn wooden crossbar that historians say weighed somewhere between 70-90 pounds strapped to the shredded muscles and exposed bone of His back, and lugging it to the top of a hill called Golgotha—or "The Place of the Skull" (Matt. 27:33).

The sober and shameful setting of Golgotha, outside the thick walls surrounding the city of Jerusalem, was where capital punishment took place in the first century because, according to Mosaic Law, dead bodies were ceremonially unclean. Plus, who wanted to have their town square—which doubled as the grocery store and community center—sullied by a crucifixion? I mean, there's no way an honorable man would want his wife or kids to witness the horror of watching someone with a crown of thorns jammed onto His head scream in agony as crude spikes were driven through His wrists and feet, then be hoisted up into the air on a cross like a human shish kebab in the heat of the day.

According to Hebrews 13:10-14, Jesus effectively carried our shame outside the city on that horrible Friday afternoon. When He chose to endure the damning reproach of Skull Mountain, it meant His followers could step out from under the deathly weight of condemnation forever.

The reason Jesus came to earth as a human—to pay the price for our sin by willingly suffering a traumatic death and separation from God so that we could be reconciled to God and be perfectly loved by Him—is the scaffolding of the Christian faith. It's the only foundation sturdy enough to hold the weight of genuine humility and compassion. Without it, healthy God-honoring and others-honoring community can't be built, much less sustained. People who don't remember the divine nature of the One who stooped to rescue them will have a very hard time bending down to help anybody else.

With the humble footwashing ceremony of John 13 and the horrible suffering Jesus endured on the Good Friday that followed in mind, I invite you to once again find a relatively quiet place where you can be alone for at least ten minutes. Then open your Bible to John 13:1-17 and slowly read through this passage again. Talk to God about what stands out to you. Tell Him whether you identify more with clumsy but genuine Peter or smoothly deceitful Judas at this point on your journey of faith. Confess where you feel like you need to be washed clean. Ask Jesus to give you the grace to be vulnerable enough to let Him take your nasty feet into His holy, nail-scarred hands.

Feel free to use the lines below to journal your prayers and how you sense the Holy Spirit guiding you with regard to being submitted to the radically humble position of allowing the Lamb of God to lower Himself for your benefit.

Below, write a responsive prayer that corresponds to the practical application of this "compassion command."

BECAUSE YOU LOWERED YOURSELF TO LOVE ME, JESUS, I WILL HUMBLE MYSELF AND LOVE:

BECAUSE YOU WALKED UP GOLGOTHA TO TAKE AWAY MY SHAME, JESUS, I'LL WALK TOWARD THIS PERSON WHO SEEMS TO SUFFER FROM SHAME:

BECAUSE YOU OPENED YOUR HANDS TO RECEIVE THE NAILS TO REDEEM ME, JESUS, I'LL USE MY HANDS TO SERVE:

# Dancing For Good

A few years after I graduated from college, I flew to California to visit my dear friend Cindy (the one who also made the adoption vow when we were in high school) and her then brand-new husband, Peter. We squealed and hugged and began telling each other stories simultaneously like we always did when we were reunited after a separation. Then she proudly gave me a tour of their first house, finishing with a flourish in the guest room where she'd thoughtfully put together a beautiful welcome basket. I remember both of us giggling, tickled over the idea that we were actually "real" adults who did adulty things like qualify for mortgages, buy cute hand towels, and curate gift baskets for overnight guests. I also vividly remember the little book with a purple cover, *Lion and Lamb*, that was in that gift basket. Cindy confided she'd bought it especially for me after someone from their young marrieds' Bible study had loaned her a copy to read.

She softly added something along the lines of, "Lease, I know you love Jesus with all your heart, but I'm not sure you believe He loves you with all of His, and I think this book can help you." Which compelled me to begin reading it that evening when I went to bed. I didn't plan on staying up all night—especially after the long, cross-country flight to get there—but I found myself so engaged with the book that I ended up finishing it just as the sun was coming up. It was written by a former Catholic priest (who left the priesthood after falling in love with his wife) and recovering alcoholic named Brennan Manning. He told riveting true stories about the kindness and accessibility of Jesus with more vulnerability than I was used to. I wasn't sure I agreed with his assertions regarding how wildly "for us" Jesus is—I'd just started working for a youth ministry and was very serious about theology—but I wanted to. And I was hooked by how he came to be known as "Brennan."

He was born Richard Francis Xavier Manning in 1934, and his best friend while growing up was a fellow named Ray Brennan. The two of them were thick as thieves who did almost everything together. They went to school together, went on double dates together, and even bought their first car together as teenagers. Of course, when the time came for them to enlist in the Korean War, they did so together. They ended up being stationed on the frontlines together, and, one snowy night in January 1952, when Richard and Ray were huddled inside a bunker just a few hundred yards from enemy lines, the unthinkable happened:

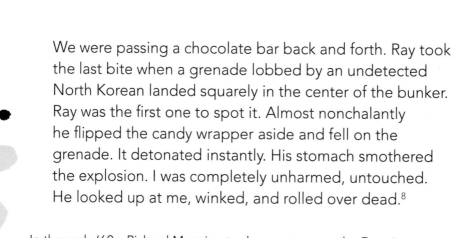

We were passing a chocolate bar back and forth. Ray took the last bite when a grenade lobbed by an undetected North Korean landed squarely in the center of the bunker. Ray was the first one to spot it. Almost nonchalantly he flipped the candy wrapper aside and fell on the grenade. It detonated instantly. His stomach smothered the explosion. I was completely unharmed, untouched. He looked up at me, winked, and rolled over dead.[8]

In the early '60s, Richard Manning took vows to enter the Franciscan priesthood. One of the requirements upon entering the priesthood was to take a saint's name as a symbol of their new identity. However, the year Mr. Manning took his vows, priests were allowed to choose their own first names. Which is how Richard Manning became Brennan Manning. The experience of losing his best friend clarified his calling and literally changed his name.

It took me many years after learning how Brennan Manning got his new name to truly connect the dots between the uncomfortable distinction of being died for and the deep comfort of knowing someone thought you were worth the sacrifice. I now believe that's the dichotomy we're called to: never forgetting we're the reason Jesus laid down His life, while always remembering He thought we were worth it. And frankly, I don't think we can hang on to the *how much more* aspect of God's love for us—much less communicate it to the lost and lonely people in our lives—unless we stay aware of how much Jesus endured on our behalf.

**Read Romans 1:1 and Philippians 1:1.**

When Paul described himself as a "servant" in the introductory remarks of these epistles, the Greek word he used was *doulos*, which is used in the New Testament "to designate a master's slave (one bound to him), but also a follower of Christ (or 'bondslave' of Christ)."[9]

**What relationships in your life would you consider yourself to be both figuratively "bound" and fully committed? Do you feel that way about your relationship with Christ? Explain.**

Read Luke 17:11-19. Why do you think Luke chose to point out the detail that the only one of ten healed lepers who turned back and thanked Jesus was also a Samaritan?

Scientific and psychological research has uncovered a plethora of proof linking gratitude with overall wellbeing. Here are a couple of statements about it: People with higher gratitude levels show more activity in the hypothalamus, which leads to improved sleep, less physical discomfort, and lower stress and anxiety.[10] And, people who practice gratitude are less vulnerable to depression.[11] What would you describe as the most obvious and immediate benefits you experience when you remember to thank God for His blessings in your life?

The eleven disciples traveled to Galilee, to the mountain where
Jesus had directed them. When they saw him, they worshiped, but
some doubted. Jesus came near and said to them,
"All authority has been given to me in heaven and on earth.
Go, therefore, and make disciples of all nations, baptizing them
in the name of the Father and of the Son and of the Holy Spirit,
teaching them to observe everything I have commanded you.
And remember, I am with you always, to the end of the age."

## MATTHEW 28:16-20

There's only one imperative in the original Greek text of this passage known
as the Great Commission—to make disciples. That's contrary to the way it's
sometimes preached, where it seems there are two different sets of emphatic
instructions from Immanuel: "go and tell" and "make disciples." However, "go"
is not a command, but one of three participles in the commission (along with
"baptizing" and "teaching"). Which means the last command our resurrected
Redeemer left us with before ascending to heaven to reign and rule at the right
hand of God the Father and intercede on our behalf was this: as you're going,
make disciples! That means we are to be making disciples in everything we do.
So it could be washing the dishes (even though one of your kids was supposed
to) or hosting a loud and opinionated relative who regularly posts obnoxious
tirades on Facebook about his or her preferred political candidate—opposite
of yours—for Thanksgiving. It could be driving across town on your only day off
to visit your aging aunt in a senior living facility, and then kneeling down to take
off her slippers in order to gently massage lotion into her cracked heels after
being tersely told by the director of the retirement home that taking care of the
residents' feet was nowhere in their nursing home aide's job description.

As Paul observed in 1 Corinthians 1, this loving-God-and-others life we've been
called to live is not normal or natural. It doesn't come naturally to squat down on
the floor (goodness knows at this age I'm not always sure I can get back up after
squatting!) and wash another person's dirty feet. Put a few dollars in the pot to
help pay for some poor soul's pedicure? Yes, I can do that. But to actually hold
a pair of nail clippers and trim down nasty talons that have yellowed and thick-
ened with age, no thank you! Nor does it come naturally to lay aside one's own
personal hopes and dreams so as to help another person attain his or hers. And
in the context of human culture, it certainly wouldn't be described as natural
to step in front of someone waiting in line for the guillotine and say, "I'd like
to take his place, Mr. Executioner." Nothing about Jesus' commands to wash

each other's feet and make disciples as we're going is natural. Instead, it's the supernatural response of those of us who've been so discombobulated by the sacrificial love of God that we just can't act "normal" anymore!

Early one recent morning, I stopped by to grab some coffee on my way to a meeting. I had a lot on my plate that day and was planning on just zipping in and zipping out of the coffee shop as fast as I could so I wouldn't be late for the next thing on my jam-packed itinerary. However, I noticed my friend Clint standing on the corner selling newspapers. Clint is part of the independent sales team for *The Contributor*, which is a bi-weekly newspaper that's only sold by men and women who've experienced the trauma of homelessness. The heart behind Street Papers (the organization that manages and facilitates *The Contributor*, which quickly became the largest selling street paper per-capita around the globe) is to provide an honest and dignified way for those who've been stigmatized by homelessness to earn a living and ultimately be able to afford permanent housing.

Clint also happens to be my favorite street preacher. We first met many years ago when I walked past him while on another coffee run and overheard him reciting long passages of Scripture. I've been stopping to have conversations with him about Jesus ever since, most of which conclude with him laying one of his huge weathered hands on my head and praying earnestly for God to guide me and bless me. Clint and I have yet to share a conversation while sitting down, much less indoors, but he's one of the first saints I asked to lay hands on Missy and pray for her after I brought her home from Haiti. He's just that special.

Anyway, despite the fact that I was in a huge hurry, I had to swing by to say hi to Clint. So I hustled over and bought a paper, gave him a big COVID-19 air hug, and then, just as I was saying goodbye and turning to walk away, he took both of my hands in his and said in his deep baritone voice, "Miss Lisa, we need to pray." At which point I thought, *Uh oh, I hope this doesn't turn into one of his sermons-disguised-as-a-prayer prayers!* It really is a wonder why God doesn't zap me with lightning sometimes.

And that's when these words came pouring out of that dear preacher's mouth: "Dear Jesus, please remind Miss Lisa that she's precious to You. Please slow her down enough today to remember how You knelt to wash Your follower's feet, and how You care so much for her that You were willing to crawl up on a cross to capture her heart. Amen."

During those few seconds Clint was praying over me, my mind flashed back to the scene in John 13. I pictured Jesus and the Twelve reclining after carbo-loading in the upper room. I could imagine Peter wearing a countenance of happy expectancy and Judas ducking his head in the hopes that neither his buddies nor the Lord would notice the shadow of betrayal on his face. Of course, Jesus knew everything. But He didn't call an attorney or press "record" on His iPhone for digital proof of the Benedict Arnold squirming before Him. He didn't stand up and pound His fist on that Passover table and then poke His finger in Judas' yellow-bellied chest and bellow, "Of all the friends I thought might stab Me in the back, I never thought it'd be You, brother!" Nope. Even though the King of all kings knew that the sins of the world were about to drain Him of His very life, He still bled grace.

I stayed there in that alfresco sanctuary for much longer than I intended to. Through Clint's oh-so-prophetic prayer, Jesus reached down with His nail-scarred hands, placed them gently on the side of my forgetful face, and tilted the attention of my mind and heart back toward the *how much more* truth of His love for me. If you've put your hope in Jesus Christ, even normal, everyday moments like going out for a cup of coffee are packed with potential for the supernatural. And we are most effective in sharing the unconditional love of God with others when we remember the cost of His personal love for us. Believers overflowing with grateful humility will give birth to community changing revivals.

One of the best dancing for good moves we can make—in light of the humility and sacrifice modeled by Jesus—is to hang on to the supernatural principles of our Savior while letting go of our natural preferences for the sake of others.

> Read 1 Chronicles 28:1-3. In this passage, David explained to the Israelites that God told him he couldn't build the temple because he was a man of war. How does that fact correlate with God's commitment to community?

Read 1 John 4:19-21. In light of this passage and John 13:34-35, what room do we have for discord and division in the body of Christ? Explain.

Read Acts 6:1-6. The first diaconate was established because there was a kink in the way the early church was distributing food to the needy widows. And the three criteria for deacons stated in this passage are: a good reputation, full of the Holy Spirit, and wisdom. Why do you think Paul said a leader needed to be filled with the Spirit to accomplish an organizational task? (Hint: it has to do with the heart of the organization.)

# Wonderful, Weighty Words

The following theological terms can help you better comprehend and communicate the *how much more* aspect of God's love, or, at the very least, help you impress folks at future dinner parties!

**KENOSIS [KUH·NOW·SUHS]:** "From the Greek root word kenóō, which means 'empty.' Kenosis is an early Christian theological term relating to the incarnation of Christ. Few Christian doctrines have been more discussed and less understood. The main cause of this difficulty lies in the mystery of the incarnation and death of the Son of God, who became a man without ceasing to be God. Great theological interest therefore has centered on Paul's declaration that the divine Christ 'emptied himself,' made Himself 'nothing' or 'no account,' when He assumed the 'form of a servant' and thus existed in the form of a man. Although the Greek word kenóō is used in this sense only in Phil. 2:7, the idea appears in 2 Cor. 8:9 in Paul's assertion, 'Though he was rich, yet for your sake he became poor, so that by his poverty you might become rich.' It may also be reflected in Jesus' description of His death upon the cross as His being 'treated with contempt' (Mark 9:12)."[12]

**ONTOLOGICAL EQUALITY:** "A phrase that describes the members of the Trinity as eternally equal in being or existence."[13] I'd like to add that they're different in function because: God the Father planned redemption and sent His Son Jesus into the world to save it (John 3:16); Jesus, the Son of God, accomplished redemption by living a perfect, sinless life and then dying on Calvary to pay the price for the sins of humankind (John 6:38); and then after Jesus died, was resurrected, and ascended into heaven, God sent the Holy Spirit to affirm redemption and empower those who put their hope in Jesus (John 14:26).

**DOCETICISM:** The term is derived from a Greek word *dokeo*, which means "to appear." This heresy—prevalent in the early church—asserted that the humanity of Jesus Christ was merely a disguise which concealed his true spiritual nature. For those who held docetic opinions, Christ only seemed to be human and only appeared to have a human body. John's gospel account counters this directly with an apologetic rooted in the fact that he had carefully observed the life and ministry of Jesus.[14]

**ANTHROPOMORPHIC:** Webster defines this as "ascribing human form or attributes to a being or thing not human, especially to a deity."[15] So when I talk about the kids in Mark 10 launching themselves into "God's lap," or when King David wrote, "When I look at your heavens, the work of your fingers" in Psalm 8, we're using anthropomorphisms to describe God from a human perspective. (Although when Jesus walked this earth as a man He did have human form and attributes.)

**GEHENNA:** "English equivalent of the Greek word (geena) derived from the Hebrew place-name (gehinnom) meaning 'valley of Hinnom,' which came to be used in New Testament times as a word for hell. The valley south of Jerusalem now called the Wadi er-Rababi (Josh. 15:8; 18:16; 2 Chron. 33:6; Jer. 32:35) became the place of child sacrifice to foreign gods. In the period between the Old and New Testament, Jewish writing used the term to describe the hell of fire in the final judgment and the New Testament uses Gehenna to speak of the place of final judgement (Matt. 5:22-29, 23:33; Mark 9:43-48; Luke 12:5)."[16]

# How Much More

## BEAUTIFUL ARE GOD'S MIRACLES UNDER A MICROSCOPE

If you then, who are evil, know how to give good gifts to your children, *how much more* will the heavenly Father give the Holy Spirit to those who ask him?

**LUKE 11:13,**
*emphasis added*

## Session Seven: THE ONLY STORY WE CAN STAKE OUR LIVES ON

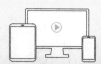

To access the video teaching sessions, use the
instructions in the back of your Bible study book.

## DISCUSSION QUESTIONS

What impacted you the most from the video teaching?

Why is it so important for us to truly understand the story of creation? How does it affect the way you see yourself? Your faith? Your witness?

Do you think most people around you find their worth and value in what God says about them or what culture says about them? Explain.

Have there been times in your life when you've distanced yourself from the Word of God? What were the consequences? How did you come back to God's life-giving Word?

How are you using the person God created and called you to be as a bridge to help people get to Jesus?

How did this video teaching reveal the redemptive heart and extravagant love of God?

What has been your biggest takeaway from this study?

How has what you've learned going to change the way you view God? How is it going to change your relationship with Him? How will it change the way you minister and share your faith?

A couple of years ago, I found myself sitting alone in a classroom at Denver Seminary with tears streaming down my cheeks. The daylong lecture had ended a few minutes earlier, and the other men and women in our doctoral candidacy program had already departed. They were anxious to grab a bite for dinner and then return to the dorm or a hotel room to work on their dissertations or slog through more required reading. I don't think anyone noticed I hadn't meandered across campus with them, chattering about what we were learning like usual. But I just couldn't make myself reenter the hustle and bustle of "normal" life quite yet. I was still in my chair, as if held in place by an invisible weight.

A few moments later, our professor—who's since become a trusted advisor as well as the de facto captain of my dissertation team—Dr. Jim Howard walked back into the classroom to pick up something he'd accidentally left on his desk. He was surprised to find me still sitting there, much less crying, and he asked if I was OK. My guess is that he was also wondering why I was pursuing a doctorate in the field of theology instead of counseling, but he was gracious and didn't verbalize that. Anyway, I don't remember exactly what I said in response to, "Are you OK?", but it was something along the lines of, "Yes sir, I'm fine. I just can't believe God is even more loving than I always hoped He was."

I kept blathering on in my gobsmacked-by-grace daze until Dr. Howard gently pulled up a chair next to me. At which point I confessed that while I'd always hoped our Creator Redeemer was perfectly, unconditionally, and immutably loving, sometimes I wasn't convinced. I couldn't help wondering how a wholly compassionate Savior could allow for systemic abuse and domestic violence and racism and global poverty and endemic food scarcity and viral pandemics and human trafficking to continue ravaging His people.

Since early adulthood, it seems a secret corner in my heart had resolutely crossed its arms and cocked an eyebrow suspiciously with regards to theodicy— to the vindication of divine goodness and providence in view of the existence of evil. And every so often it piped up with an obstinate question like, *If God's entirely loving, then why doesn't He step up to the plate and lock up all the human traffickers, pedophiles, drug dealers, rapists, and murderers in an old, windowless, efficiency apartment with a pack of hungry hyenas with irritable bowel syndrome?*

However, that resistant corner of my heart began uncrossing its arms as we discussed how the Bible is not simply scriptural data but is the grand story of

God's redemptive movement in human history. Even the most problematic passages—those that can be extremely difficult to understand from our current cultural context—ultimately point to our Creator Redeemer's kindness.

In the years since my conversation with Dr. Howard, I've become absolutely convinced that the following three hermeneutical principles he taught our class (and teaches at conferences and churches around the world) can help everyone—from seekers to saints—better understand, interpret, apply, and appreciate Scripture, even the trickiest of texts:

1. Scripture reveals that God is always in the process of mitigating evil.

2. Scripture reveals that God is always in the process of restoring human dignity.

3. Scripture reveals that God is always in the process of pointing us toward the "true north" of Jesus Christ.

Therefore, in this last session we have to hang out together, I thought we'd review some of the key passages we've explored during this *How Much More* journey and practice applying those three principles. So here we go!

## Session One Review

Let's start with those two texts from the very beginning about the Sabbath that I used to think were belly button prohibition passages.

> Read the following passages, then consider: If you were having a conversation with someone who presumes the Bible is boring, or a rigid book of rules, or maybe they don't yet have a real relationship with Jesus, how would you use your answers to the questions that follow the biblical texts to explain that these verses are promissory instead of punitive?

> "Remember the Sabbath day, to keep it holy: You are to labor six days and do all your work, but the seventh day is a Sabbath to the LORD your God. You must not do any work—you, your

son or daughter, your male or female servant, your livestock, or the resident alien who is within your city gates. For the LORD made the heavens and the earth, the sea, and everything in them in six days; then he rested on the seventh day. Therefore the LORD blessed the Sabbath day and declared it holy."

**EXODUS 20:8-11**

The LORD spoke to Moses: "Speak to the Israelites and tell them: These are my appointed times, the times of the LORD that you will proclaim as sacred assemblies. Work may be done for six days, but on the seventh day there is to be a Sabbath of complete rest, a sacred assembly. You are not to do any work; it is a Sabbath to the LORD wherever you live."

**LEVITICUS 23:1-3**

How do these passages reveal that God is always in the process of mitigating evil?

How do these passages reveal that God is always in the process of restoring human dignity?

How do these passages reveal that God is always in the process of pointing us toward the "true north" of Jesus Christ?

What fresh insights did God give you about honoring the Sabbath through this study?

## Session Two Review

The texts we perused in Session Two initially appeared a bit more complicated than a potential bikini ban. They relate to the practice of slavery, a gut-wrenching subject most of us would rather shove under the proverbial rug than peer at up close. And yet, once again, God's redemptive plan for humanity pierces through the cultural darkness of these passage just as surely as daffodils poke through the cold, hard soil of winter as harbingers of spring!

So, as before, read the following passages, then consider: If you were having a conversation with someone who presumes the Bible is boring, or a rigid book of rules, or maybe they don't yet have a real relationship with Jesus, how would you use your answers to the questions that follow the biblical texts to explain that these verses are promissory instead of punitive?

"When you buy a Hebrew slave, he is to serve for six years; then in the seventh he is to leave as a free man without paying anything. ..."

"When a man strikes his male or female slave with a rod, and the slave dies under his abuse, the owner must be punished. However, if the slave can stand up after a day or two, the owner should not be punished because he is his owner's property. ..."

"When an ox gores a man or a woman to death, the ox must be stoned, and its meat may not be eaten, but the ox's owner is innocent. However, if the ox was in the habit of goring, and its owner has been warned yet does not restrain it, and it kills a man or a woman, the ox must be stoned, and its owner must also be put to death. If instead a ransom is demanded of him, he can pay a redemption price for his life in the full amount demanded from him. If it gores a son or a daughter, he is to be dealt with according to this same law. If the ox gores a male or female slave, he must give thirty shekels of silver to the slave's master, and the ox must be stoned."

**EXODUS 21:2,20-21,28-32**

"If your fellow Hebrew, a man or woman, is sold to you and serves you six years, you must set him free in the seventh year. When you set him free, do not send him away empty-handed. Give generously to him from your flock, your threshing floor, and your winepress. You are to give him whatever the LORD your God has blessed you with. Remember that you were a slave in the land of Egypt and the LORD your God redeemed you; that is why I am giving you this command today. But if your slave says to you, 'I don't want to leave you,' because he loves you and your family, and is well off with you, take an awl and pierce through his ear into the door, and he will become your slave for life. Also treat your female slave the same way. Do not regard it as a hardship when you set him free, because he worked for you six years—worth twice the wages of a hired worker. Then the LORD your God will bless you in everything you do."

**DEUTERONOMY 15:12-18**

"Do not return a slave to his master when he has escaped from his master to you. Let him live among you wherever he wants within your city gates. Do not mistreat him."

**DEUTERONOMY 23:15-16**

"If a man is discovered kidnapping one of his Israelite brothers, whether he treats him as a slave or sells him, the kidnapper must die. You must purge the evil from you."

**DEUTERONOMY 24:7**

How do these passages reveal that God is always in the process of mitigating evil?

How do these passages reveal that God is always in the process of restoring human dignity?

How do these passages reveal that God is always in the process of pointing us toward the "true north" of Jesus Christ?

What fresh insights did God give you about the inherent value of all people through this study?

## Session Three Review

What with all the Holy Spirit's tutoring to correct my misperceptions about Sabbath and slavery in Scripture, the unlikely love story of a preacher and a prostitute in Session Three provided a really refreshing reprieve. I hope you enjoyed reading my wildly informal paraphrase of that historical and meta-phorical romance as much as I enjoyed writing it! I've always been a sucker for a good love story. And in my biased opinion, Hollywood's got nothing on the Bible. Even Julia Roberts and Richard Gere pale in comparison to Gomer and Hosea. Which means the hermeneutical exercise we're trying to ingrain as a habit should be relatively easy this go 'round.

> Read the following passages, then consider: If you were having a conversation with someone who presumes the Bible is boring, or a rigid book of rules, or maybe they think Jesus is a "righteous prophet" like Ghandi or Buddha but not the Redeemer of the world, how would you use your answers to the questions that follow the biblical texts to explain why God prompted a really good guy to propose to a really bad girl, marry her, and then redeem his estranged wife after she'd betrayed him?

> The first time God spoke to Hosea he said: "Find a whore and marry her. Make this whore the mother of your children. And here's why: This whole country has become a whorehouse, unfaithful to me, God."

### HOSEA 1:2, MSG

> After Gomer had weaned Lo-ruhamah, she again became pregnant and gave birth to a second son. And the Lord said, "Name him Lo-ammi—'Not my people'—for Israel is not my people, and I am not their God."

### HOSEA 1:8-9, NLT

Yes, their mother is promiscuous; she conceived them and acted shamefully. For she thought, "I will follow my lovers, the men who give me my food and water, my wool and flax, my oil and drink."

**HOSEA 2:5**

"On the very same day, I'll answer"—this is GOD's Message—"I'll answer the sky, sky will answer earth, Earth will answer grain and wine and olive oil, and they'll all answer Jezreel. I'll plant her in the good earth. I'll have mercy on No-Mercy. I'll say to Nobody, 'You're my dear Somebody,' and he'll say 'You're my God!'"

**HOSEA 2:21-23, MSG**

Then the Lord said to me, "Go, and get your wife again and bring her back to you and love her, even though she loves adultery. For the Lord still loves Israel though she has turned to other gods and offered them choice gifts." So I bought her back from her slavery for a couple of dollars and eight bushels of barley, and I said to her, "You must live alone for many days; do not go out with other men nor be a prostitute, and I will wait for you."

**HOSEA 3:1-3, TLB**

How does this Bible story reveal that God is always in the process of mitigating evil?

How does this Bible story reveal that God is always in the process of restoring human dignity?

How does this Bible story reveal that God is always in the process of pointing us toward the "true north" of Jesus Christ?

What fresh insights did God give you about His unconditional love through this study?

## Session Four Review

My guess is that some of you may have felt a wee bit disappointed at the beginning of Session Four. After finally making it to the New Testament, instead of getting to enjoy a feel-good story with a happy ending—like Jesus healing some leprous daddy just in time for him to make it to his son's Little League game— we get mired in an eschatologically-themed parable about five procrastinating chicks who got bounced from a wedding party. But once again, even the tales that read like warning labels in God's story ultimately point to the amazing grace of the gospel, pointing to a merciful Savior who longs to rescue, redeem, and restore sinners, giving us chance after chance to accept His invitation. So let's step up to the plate and take another swing.

> Read the following passages, then consider: If you were having a conversation with someone who presumes the Bible is boring, or a rigid book of rules, or maybe they perceive Jesus to be "a" way to be reconciled to God instead of "the" way, how would you use your answers to the questions that follow the parable to explain that this bridesmaids tale paints a picture of an accessible Savior who invites us to know Him?

"At that time the kingdom of heaven will be like ten virgins who took their lamps and went out to meet the groom. Five of them were foolish and five were wise. When the foolish took their lamps, they didn't take oil with them; but the wise ones took oil in their flasks with their lamps. When the groom was delayed, they all became drowsy and fell asleep. In the middle of the night there was a shout: 'Here's the groom! Come out to meet him.' Then all the virgins got up and trimmed their lamps. The foolish ones said to the wise ones, 'Give us some of your oil, because our lamps are going out.' The wise ones answered, 'No, there won't be enough for us and for you. Go instead to those who sell oil, and buy some for yourselves.' When they had gone to buy some, the groom arrived, and those who were ready went in with him to the wedding banquet, and the door was shut. Later the rest of the virgins also came and said, 'Master, master, open up for us!' He replied, 'Truly I tell you, I don't know you!' Therefore be alert, because you don't know either the day or the hour."

**MATTHEW 25:1-13**

How does this parable reveal that God is always in the process of mitigating evil?

How does this parable reveal that God is always in the process of restoring human dignity?

How does this parable reveal that God is always in the process of pointing us toward the "true north" of Jesus Christ?

What fresh insights did God give you about being spiritually alert and having an urgency to share the living hope of Jesus Christ through this study?

## Session Five Review

I must confess, Session Five wrecked me. I finished it in the middle of the night, but instead of going to bed, I walked into the living room and sat on the couch and cried. I confessed to God how sorry I was for each and every time I hadn't turned to the *eperchomai* reality of His Spirit for comfort during the chaos and turbulence and loss of 2020. How sometimes I foolishly and faithlessly forget how incredibly close to us He is. And because tears of repentance usually soften our hearts into the posture of praise, I soon found myself overwhelmed with gratitude. I profusely thanked Him for turning my dry bones of grief and disappointment into a dance of renewed dependency on His grace. I completely lost track of time during that personal revival until I noticed light coming through the windows—the sun was coming up in the loveliest hues of orange and yellow. It's almost as if our Creator Redeemer was winking at me and whispering fondly, "I know your memory tends to be a bit spotty, Honey, so here's another tangible reminder of how I can bring vibrancy out of void."

I love the familiar promise in Jeremiah, "You will seek me and find me when you search for me with all your heart" (29:13). But the older I get—and the more aware I become of my proclivity to miss the nearness of God's Spirit—the more I appreciate the audacious kindness He lavishes on those of us who've been disengaged.

> "I was sought by those who did not ask; I was found by those who did not seek me. I said, 'Here I am, here I am,' to a nation that did not call on my name."

## ISAIAH 65:1

My hope is that God used all of the passages we contemplated in Session Five to wreck your heart in a redemptive way. To remind you that because of Him, our nothing special can become something supernatural.

In light of that transformative truth, consider how you would use our now familiar hermeneutical principles reflected in the questions that follow this text to explain the following miraculous *eperchomai* encounters in Luke and Acts to someone who presumes the Bible is boring, or a rigid book of rules, or maybe assumes he or she is not "good enough" for God.

In the sixth month, the angel Gabriel was sent by God to a town in Galilee called Nazareth, to a virgin engaged to a man named Joseph, of the house of David. The virgin's name was Mary. And the angel came to her and said, "Greetings, favored woman! The Lord is with you." But she was deeply troubled by this statement, wondering what kind of greeting this could be. Then the angel told her, "Do not be afraid, Mary, for you have found favor with God. Now listen: You will conceive and give birth to a son, and you will name him Jesus. He will be great and will be called the Son of the Most High, and the Lord God will give him the throne of his father David. He will reign over the house of Jacob forever, and his kingdom will have no end." Mary asked the angel, "How can this be, since

I have not had sexual relations with a man?"
The angel replied to her, "*The Holy Spirit will come upon you,*
and the power of the Most High will overshadow you. Therefore,
the holy one to be born will be called the Son of God. And
consider your relative Elizabeth—even she has conceived a
son in her old age, and this is the sixth month for her who was
called childless. For nothing will be impossible with God."

### LUKE 1:26-37, EMPHASIS MINE

While he was with them, he commanded them not to leave
Jerusalem, but to wait for the Father's promise. "Which," he said,
"you have heard me speak about; for John baptized with water,
but you will be baptized with the Holy Spirit in a few days."
So when they had come together, they asked him, "Lord,
are you restoring the kingdom to Israel at this time?"
He said to them, "It is not for you to know times or
periods that the Father has set by his own authority. But
you will receive power *when the Holy Spirit has come
on you*, and you will be my witnesses in Jerusalem, in all
Judea and Samaria, and to the ends of the earth."

### ACTS 1:4-8, EMPHASIS MINE

How do these *eperchomai* encounters help reveal that God is always in
the process of mitigating evil?

How do these *eperchomai* encounters help reveal that God is always in
the process of restoring human dignity?

How do these *eperchomai* encounters help reveal that God is always in the process of pointing us toward the "true north" of Jesus Christ?

What fresh insights did God give you about His desire to transform your nothing special into something supernatural through this study?

## Session Six Review

Now to the last—but I certainly hope not the least!—session to review. Session Six could be voted "Most Likely to Come in Handy During Church Dinner Party Conversations." It's the one where we used that fancy Greek term, *homoousios*, which means "same in substance"—to explain the orthodox doctrine (adopted at the Council of Nicea) that Jesus the Son shares the very same substance and nature as God the Father and is in no way inferior. A fact that makes the scene at the last supper, when King Jesus chose to squat down, pick up a towel, and wash the nasty feet of those disciples—including Judas—all the more stunning.

How does the portrait of divine humility and sacrificial compassion revealed below in John 13 both illustrate and, in some sense, fulfill the key hermeneutical principles reflected in the questions that follow?

Before the Passover Festival, Jesus knew that his hour had come to depart from this world to the Father. Having loved his own who were in the world, he loved them to the end. Now when it was time for supper, the devil had already put it into the heart of Judas, Simon Iscariot's son, to betray him. Jesus knew that the Father had given everything into his hands, that he had come from God, and that he was going back to God. So he got up from supper, laid aside his outer clothing, took a towel, and tied it around himself. Next, he poured water into a basin and began to wash his disciples' feet and to dry them with the towel tied around him.

He came to Simon Peter, who asked him, "Lord, are you going to wash my feet?"

Jesus answered him, "What I'm doing you don't realize now, but afterward you will understand."

"You will never wash my feet," Peter said.

Jesus replied, "If I don't wash you, you have no part with me."

Simon Peter said to him, "Lord, not only my feet, but also my hands and my head."

"One who has bathed," Jesus told him, "doesn't need to wash anything except his feet, but he is completely clean. You are clean, but not all of you." For he knew who would betray him. This is why he said, "Not all of you are clean."

When Jesus had washed their feet and put on his outer clothing, he reclined again and said to them, "Do you know what I have done for you? You call me Teacher and Lord—and you are speaking rightly, since that is what I am. So if I, your Lord and Teacher, have washed your feet, you also ought to wash one another's feet. For I have given you an example, that you also should do just as I have done for you. Truly I tell you, a servant is not greater than his master, and a messenger is not greater than the one who sent him. If you know these things, you are blessed if you do them."

**JOHN 13:1-17**

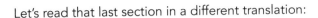

Let's read that last section in a different translation:

> After washing their feet, he put his robe on and returned to his place at the table. "Do you understand what I just did?" Jesus said. "You've called me your teacher and lord, and you're right, for that's who I am. So if I'm your teacher and lord and have just washed your dirty feet, then you should follow the example that I've set for you and wash one another's dirty feet. Now do for each other what I have just done for you. I speak to you timeless truth: a servant is not superior to his master, and an apostle is never greater than the one who sent him. So now put into practice what I have done for you, and you will experience a life of happiness enriched with untold blessings!"

### JOHN 13:12-17, TPT

> "I give you a new command: Love one another. Just as I have loved you, you are also to love one another. By this everyone will know that you are my disciples, if you love one another."

### JOHN 13:34-35

How does the humility and sacrificial compassion Jesus displayed in John 13 reveal that God is always in the process of mitigating evil?

How does the humility and sacrificial compassion Jesus displayed in John 13 reveal that God is always in the process of restoring human dignity?

How does the humility and sacrificial compassion Jesus displayed in John 13 reveal the "true north" God has been pointing to since the beginning of human history?

What fresh insights did God give you about Jesus' sacrificial love for you through this study?

My precious mom, Patti Angel (yes, that really is my phenom-of-a-free-throw-shooter mama's last name!), who introduced me to Jesus, is eighty-three years young and is a wonderful example of the ever-increasing love and liberty that should define followers of Christ. Because of COVID-19, Missy and I weren't able to spend as much time as we normally do with her this past year (she still lives in Central Florida, where I grew up). So it was a huge treat when my nephew, John Michael, drove her up to spend two weeks with us this Christmas. We had the best time playing games, staying up late telling stories, and tromping through the early January snow that blanketed "Missy's Mountain." Mom even good-naturedly crawled onto a sled with John Michael and whooped it up while barreling down a steep slope on the backside of our property!

I don't have many childhood memories that include the kind of silliness and giggle fits we experienced with Mom recently. Back when I was Missy's age, Mom was pretty bound up. She was much more concerned about adhering to the strict behavioral guidelines that came from the Good Book—things like not dancing or playing cards or wearing too much jewelry or letting her little girls wear bikinis in the privacy of their own backyard on Sunday afternoons—than she was about sharing belly laughs. My precious mama had been taught by well-intentioned spiritual leaders that being a "good Christian" was more about what you couldn't do than what you could. Therefore, before I even learned to read, I'd learned to revere that big, black, leather-bound King James Bible, which stood on the most prominent shelf in our living room. What it took me much longer to learn is that living book is not legalistic or archaic literature but a supernatural love story.

When I was Missy's age, I used to watch my lovely mother walk elegantly across a room and think, *I hope one day I'll be as beautiful as her.* And I had a similar thought recently while watching her and Missy with their heads bent together, murmuring happily about something they thought was funny in a bedtime story. Only now, I hope one day to have a heart that's as beautifully bent toward God and others as my mom's is. The decades of following God—even when she unwittingly stumbled down paths that He hadn't paved and had to be guided back to His redemptive route by the Holy Spirit—have weathered her soul into a gorgeous patina of trust. She's become like Caleb, whose wholehearted faith in God increased exponentially as he aged, so much so that he began another exciting and challenging chapter of ministry when he was eighty-five years old:

I was forty years old when Moses, the servant of the LORD, sent me from Kadesh-barnea to explore the land of Canaan. I returned and gave an honest report, but my brothers who went with me frightened the people from entering the Promised Land. For my part, *I wholeheartedly followed the LORD my God.* So that day Moses solemnly promised me, "The land of Canaan on which you were just walking will be your grant of land and that of your descendants forever, because *you wholeheartedly followed the LORD my God.*" Now, as you can see, the LORD has kept me alive and well as he promised for all these forty-five years since Moses made this promise—even while Israel wandered in the wilderness. Today I am eighty-five years old. I am as strong now as I was when Moses sent me on that journey, and I can still travel and fight as well as I could then. So give me the hill country that the LORD promised me. You will remember that as scouts we found the descendants of Anak living there in great, walled towns. But if the LORD is with me, I will drive them out of the land, just as the LORD said." So Joshua blessed Caleb son of Jephunneh and gave Hebron to him as his portion of land. Hebron still belongs to the descendants of Caleb son of Jephunneh the Kenizzite because *he wholeheartedly followed the L*ORD, *the God of Israel.*

**JOSHUA 14:7-14, NLT, EMPHASIS MINE**

Wouldn't it be incredible if that's how we were described too, as someone who wholeheartedly follows the Lord? And may it be even more true of us after this how much more adventure we've taken together!

# NOTES

LEADER GUIDE

# How Much More

## Session One

1. Welcome participants to the study of *How Much More*. Use the following questions to prompt discussion in your group:

   - What drew you to this study of *How Much More*?

   - What three words would you use to describe your relationship with God? Why did you choose those three?

   - When you hear the words "extravagant love," what comes to mind? Do you believe that God has extravagant love for you? If so, how do you experience it? If not, why not?

   - What is one thing you hope to gain from this study?

2. Play the Session One video teaching. (You can access the videos on the card at the back of the Bible study book.)

3. Following the video, use the questions on page 9 to discuss the video teaching.

4. Close the session in prayer, asking God to open the hearts of your group members to know God more deeply and truly understand how much He loves each one.

## Session Two

1. Greet participants and welcome them back to the study of *How Much More*. Use the following questions to prompt discussion about last week's personal study:

   - What was the most significant thing you learned from your personal study this week?

   - Before this session, how would you have defined Sabbath? How has that definition changed?

   - What is a "redemptive fence"? What redemptive fences have you run into lately?

   - What is some inherited theology you've had to unlearn? How was this theology hindering your relationship with God?

   - Why is Sabbath important to our relationship with God and ministry for Him? What is your current experience with carving out space to be alone with God and rest? What can you do to enhance this?

   - How did you see God's extravagant love in what you studied this week?

2. Play the Session Two video teaching.

3. Following the video, use the questions on page 35 to discuss the video teaching.

4. Form participants into groups of three and four and instruct them to share with each other how God has protected them and shown them that He is for them. Encourage one person in each group to close with prayer.

## Session Three

1. Welcome participants back to the study of *How Much More*. Use the following questions to prompt discussion about last week's personal study:

- What was the most significant thing you learned from your personal study this week?

- How did the passages you studied about slavery this week show you the redemptive heart of God?

- Why do the timeless principles of Scripture move forward but some of the practices chronicled in the Bible do not? How would you explain this to someone unfamiliar with the Bible?

- How has God used this session to speak to you about racial and ethnic discrimination?

- In light of what you've learned, what is God prompting you to do? What will be your first step?

- How did you see God's extravagant love in what you studied this week?

2. Play the Session Three video teaching.

3. Following the video, use the questions on page 59 to discuss the video teaching.

4. As you close the session, provide time for participants to meditate on the love and affection God has for them, then encourage them to pray, thanking God for His extravagant love.

## Session Four

1. Welcome participants back to the study of *How Much More*. Use the following questions to prompt discussion about last week's personal study:

- What was the most significant thing you learned from your personal study this week?

- How do you see the heart of God in Hosea's story?

- What things of the world are you most prone to run after instead of pursuing God?

- How can recognizing our own weakness and incapacities actually help us see God's love exponentially bigger and clearer?

- How has God redeemed the ugly parts of your story?

- How did you see God's extravagant love in what you studied this week?

2. Play the Session Four video teaching.

3. Following the video, use the questions on page 85 to discuss the video teaching.

4. Close the session by asking for volunteers to share some long-term

prayer requests. Remind the group of the goodness of the Father to give good gifts to His children. Then lead group members to intercede on behalf of those who shared their concerns.

## Session Five

1. Welcome participants back to the study of *How Much More*. Use the following questions to prompt discussion about last week's personal study:

   - What was the most significant thing you learned from your personal study this week?

   - How has waiting on the Lord been a part of your faith journey? What did He teach you in the waiting?

   - How have you grown sleepy in your relationship with Jesus? What's the loudest spiritual wake-up call you've ever received?

   - Are you currently running toward the lost with the good news of Jesus? If so, how? If not, why not?

   - How did you see God's extravagant love in what you studied this week?

2. Play the Session Five video teaching.

3. Following the video, use the questions on page 111 to discuss the video teaching.

4. As you close the session, lead a prayer thanking God for calling and equipping His daughters for ministry. Ask Him to continue to open doors and provide opportunities to use your giftedness for His glory.

## Session Six

1. Welcome participants back to the study of *How Much More*. Use the following questions to prompt discussion about last week's personal study:

   - What was the most significant thing you learned from your personal study this week?

   - Has God ever asked you to do something that seemed impossible? Explain.

   - What has God done recently in your life or your church that has amazed you?

   - In recent days, how has the Holy Spirit ministered to you and also empowered you to accomplish God's work?

   - How has God brought life out of a painful loss in your life?

   - How did you see God's extravagant love in what you studied this week?

2. Play the Session Six video teaching.

3. Following the video, use the questions on page 137 to discuss the video teaching.

4. Close the session with a time of thanksgiving for Jesus, the living Word, who knows us, sees us, and loves us; and for Scripture, the written Word, the beautiful love story given to us by God so that we might know Him.

## Session Seven

1. Welcome participants back to the study of *How Much More*. Use the following questions to prompt discussion about last week's personal study:

   - What was the most significant thing you learned from your personal study this week?

   - What was Jesus teaching His disciples by washing their feet?

   - What does it mean to be a servant? Is it easy or hard for you to serve others? Explain.

   - How do you balance considering others more highly than yourself with healthy self-care?

   - How does being a servant show the how much more love of God? Who is someone you need to serve this week?

   - How did you see God's extravagant love in what you studied this week?

2. Play the Session Seven video teaching.

3. Following the video, use the questions on page 161 to discuss the video teaching.

4. Thank your group members for participating in this study. Close with a season of prayer, inviting participants to thank God for what they've learned in the study and for showering us with His extravagant love.

# ENDNOTES

## Session One

1. Merriam Webster s.v. "peruse," accessed February 22, 2021, https://www.merriam-webster.com/dictionary/peruse.
2. "Sabbath," *The Anchor Yale Bible Dictionary* (New York, NY: Doubleday, 1992), 849.
3. Rodney Cooper, *Holman New Testament Commentary: Mark*, vol. 2 (Nashville, TN: Broadman and Holman Publishers, 2000).
4. Donald K. McKim, *The Westminster Dictionary of Theological Terms, Second Edition, Revised and Expanded* (Louisville, KY: Westminster John Knox Press, 2014), 1.
5. *Ibid.*
6. *Tabletalk Magazine*, July 2005: "Imago Dei" (Lake Mary, FL: Ligonier Ministries, 2005), 5.
7. Stanley J. Grenz and Jay T. Smith, *Pocket Dictionary of Ethics* (Downers Grove, IL: InterVarsity Press, 2003), 94.
8. "Sabbath," *The Anchor Yale Bible Dictionary*, 850.

## Session Two

1. Jemar Tisby, *The Color of Compromise* (Grand Rapids, MI: Zondervan; 2019), 39.
2. Eugene H. Merrill, *New American Commentary: Deuteronomy*, vol. 4 (Nashville, TN: B&H Publishing Group, 2012).
3. G. K. Chesterton, *Tremendous Trifles* (New York, NY: Dodd, Mead & Co. 1910), 315.
4. "Exegesis," *The Anchor Yale Bible Dictionary*.

5. "Hermeneutics," *The Anchor Yale Bible Dictionary*.
6. Wayne Grudem, *Systematic Theology* (Grand Rapids, MI: Zondervan, 1994), 90.
7. William Webb, *Slaves, Women and Homosexuals: Exploring the Hermeneutics of Cultural Analysis* (Downers Grove, IL: InterVarsity Press, 2001).
8. *Ibid.*

## Session Three

1. Information for this graphic taken from *Biblical Illustrator*. https://s7d9.scene7.com/is/content/LifeWayChristianResources/biblical-illustrator-time-line_20191031pdf.pdf
2. James E. Smith, *Old Testament Survey Series: The Minor Prophets* (Joplin, MO:The. College Press, 2013).
3. Charles Dickens, *A Tale of Two Cities* (London, England: James Nisbet & Co., 1902).
4. "Hosea," Strong's H1954, *Blue Letter Bible online*. Available at blueletterbible.org.
5. Gordon D. Fee and Robert L. Hubbard Jr. eds., *The Eerdmans Companion to the Bible* (Grand Rapids, MI: Wm B. Eerdmans Publishing Company, 2011).
6. *Ibid.*

## Session Four

1. Eugene E. Carpenter and Philip W. Comfort, *Holman Treasury of Key Bible Words: 200 Greek and 200 Hebrew Words Defined and Explained* (Nashville, TN: B&H Publishing Group, 2000).
2. Craig Blomberg, *New American Commentary: Matthew*, vol. 22

(Nashville, TN: B&H Publishing Group, 2012).

3. William Hendriksen, *Baker New Testament Commentary* (Grand Rapids, MI: Baker Academic, 2013).

4. Klyne R Snodgrass, *Stories with Intent: A Comprehensive Guide to the Parables of Jesus* (Grand Rapids, MI: Wm B. Eerdmans Publishing Company, 2018), 509.

5. James Montgomery Boice, *Boice Expositional Commentary: Matthew* (Grand Rapids, MI: Baker Books, 2013).

6. *Ibid.*

7. Alan Wright, *Lover of My Soul* (Colorado Springs, CO: Multnomah Books, 1998), 83.

8. *Ibid.*, 82.

9. Charles Spurgeon, *Spurgeon's Verse Expositions of the Bible: Hebrews.* Available at studylight.org.

10. *Stories with Intent: A Comprehensive Guide to the Parables of Jesus.*

11. C. S. Lewis, *The Weight of Glory* (New York, NY: Harper Collins, 1949), 45.

12. Jon Krakauer, *Into the Wild* (New York, NY: Anchor Books, 1997).

13. *Ibid.*

14. *Ibid.*

15. Elisabeth Elliot, *A Path Through Suffering* (Grand Rapids, MI: Baker Books, 1990).

16. Craig Blomberg, *Interpreting the Parables* (Downers Grove, IL: InterVarsity Press, 1990), 326-327.

17. "Parable," *The Anchor Yale Bible Dictionary,* 146.

18. "Synoptic Gospels," *Baker Encyclopedia of the Bible* (Grand Rapids, MI: Baker Book House, 1988).

19. "Kerygma," *Evangelical Dictionary of Theology* (Grand Rapids, MI: Baker Books, 1984).

20. "Eschatology," *New Unger's Bible Dictionary* (Chicago, IL: Moody Press, 2013).

21. "Parousia," *The Anchor Yale Bible Dictionary,* 166.

## Session Five

1. Horst Robert Balz and Gerhard Schneider, *Exegetical Dictionary of the New Testament* (Grand Rapids, MI: Wm B. Eerdmans Publishing Company, 1990), 135.

2. J. Reiling and J. L. Swellengrebel, *A Handbook on the Gospel of Luke, UBS Handbook Series* (New York: United Bible Societies, 1993), 59.

3. "Parakletos," Strong's G3875, *Blue Letter Bible online.* Available at blueletterbible.org.

4. Lisa Harper, *Believing Jesus: Are You Willing to Risk Everything? A Journey Through the Book of Acts* (Nashville, TN: Thomas Nelson, 2015), 26.

5. "History of the Dahlia," Floom.com, accessed February 23, 2021, https://www.floom.com/magazine/article/flower-of-the-month-dahlia.

6. Dictionary.com s.v. "pantheon," accessed February 23, 2021, https://www.dictionary.com/browse/pantheon.

7. "Polytheism, Greco-Roman," *Dictionary of New Testament Background: A Compendium of Contemporary Biblical Scholarship* (Downers Grove, IL: InterVarsity Press, 2000), 815.

8. Kelly M. Kapic and Wesley Vander Lugt, *Pocket Dictionary of the Reformed Tradition* (Downers Grove, IVP Academic, 2013), 87.

9. Donald K. McKim, *The Westminster Dictionary of Theological Terms* (Louisville, KY: Westminster John Knox Press, 2014), 339.

10. Sinclair Ferguson, *The Holy Spirit* (Downers Grove, IL: IVP Academic, 1996), 16.

11. F. F. Bruce, *The New Testament International Commentary on the New Testament: The Book of Acts* (Grand Rapids, MI: Wm B. Eerdmans Publishing Company, 1988), 49-50.

## Session Six

1. Bruce L. Shelley, "The First Council of Nicea (325)," ChristianityToday.com, accessed February 23, 2021, https://www.christianitytoday.com/history/issues/issue-28/325-first-council-of-nicea.html.

2. Stanley J. Grenz, David Guretzki, and Cherith Fee Nordling, *Pocket Dictionary of Theological Terms* (Downers Grove, IL: InterVarsity Press, 1999), 60–61.

3. Stephen J. Nichols, *For Us and for Our Salvation* (Wheaton, IL: Crossway, 2007), 68.

4. J. I Packer, Evangelism and the Sovereignty of God (Downers Grove, IL: InterVarsity Press, 2012), 29.

5. D. A. Carson, *The Pillar New Testament Commentary: The Gospel according to John* (Grand Rapids, MI: Wm B. Eerdmans Publishing Company, 1991), 467–468.

6. *Ibid.*, 462.

7. "Hypodeigma," Strong's G5262, *Blue Letter Bible online.* Available at blueletterbible.org.

8. Brennan Manning, from remarks at First Presbyterian Church, Winston-Salem, NC, Nov. 18-20, 1990, as told in Alan Wright's book, *Lover of My Soul.*

9. "Servant, Service," *Evangelical Dictionary of Biblical Theology*, electronic ed. (Grand Rapids: Baker Book House, 1996), 725.

10. Paula Felps, "Brain Matters: Mindfulness Can Change The Way You Think, How You Feel," as found in Lisa Harper, *The Sacrament of Happy* (Nashville, TN: B&H Publishing, 2017).

11. *Ibid.*

12. "Kenosis," *The International Standard Bible Encyclopedia, Revised* (Grand Rapids, MI: Wm. B. Eerdmans Publishing Company, 1988), 7-8.

13. *Systematic Theology*, 1250.

14. *The Apologetics Study Bible: Real Questions, Straight Answers, Stronger Faith* (Nashville, TN: Holman Bible Publishers, 2007), 1865.

15. "Anthropomorphic," *Webster's Encyclopedic Unabridged Dictionary of the English Language* (San Diego, CA: Thunder Bay Press, 2001), 88.

16. "Gehenna," *Holman Illustrated Bible Dictionary* (Nashville, TN: Holman Bible Publishers, 2003), 631.

I'd also like to acknowledge another professor and theologian, Dr. William J. Webb. I've never had the privilege of sitting directly under Dr. Webb's teaching, but his books have helped reinvigorate my love for God's Word.

# CHECK OUT THESE BOOKS
## by
# LISA HARPER

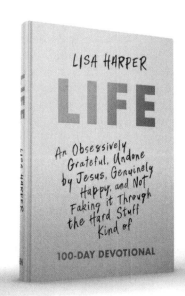

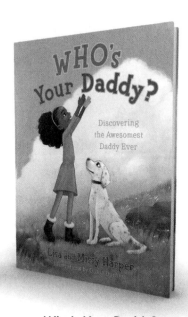

**The Sacrament of Happy**
What a Smiling God Brings
to a Wounded World

**LIFE**
An Obsessively Grateful, Undone
by Jesus, Genuinely Happy, and
Not Faking it Through the Hard
Stuff Kind of 100-Day Devotional

**Who's Your Daddy?**
Discovering the Awesomest
Daddy Ever

For kids ages 4-8

AVAILABLE EVERYWHERE BOOKS ARE SOLD

# *Additional Studies from Lisa Harper*

## JOB
7 Sessions

Discover some radically redemptive facets of pain and suffering while you learn how to engage with and authentically embrace the wounded world around you through the unlikely hope and joy that permeate even the hardest moments in Job's story.

lifeway.com/job

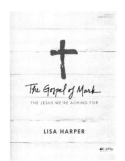

## THE GOSPEL OF MARK
7 Sessions

Explore the action-packed Gospel of Mark—the first literary compilation of Jesus' earthly life and ministry—to lean further into His divine compassion in a way that might just change your life forever!

lifeway.com/gospelofmark

## HEBREWS
7 Sessions

Journey through the Book of Hebrews for an eye-opening and encouraging experience to help increase your intimacy with Jesus and deepen your faith in Him. He'll teach you not to falter when faced with personal difficulties or cultural persecution.

lifeway.com/hebrews

**lifeway.com/lisaharper**
800.458.2772

Lifeway women

# Get the most from your study.

**COMPANION PRODUCTS**

**DVD Set,** includes 7 video teaching sessions from Lisa Harper, each approximately 30–40 minutes

**IN THIS STUDY, YOU'LL:**

- Tackle some overlooked or misunderstood passages in Scripture, uncovering how they actually amplify the love and goodness of God.

- Explore the historical-cultural context of biblical texts to grasp their deeper meaning.

- Discover God's redemptive heart throughout Scripture and how He longs to redeem you.

- Allow a renewed understanding of God's perfect compassion and perfect holiness to drive you to deeper intimacy and trust in Him.

To enrich your study experience, consider the accompanying *How Much More* video teaching sessions, approximately 30–40 minutes each, from Lisa Harper.

**STUDYING ON YOUR OWN?**

Watch Lisa Harper's teaching sessions, available via redemption code for individual video-streaming access, printed in this Bible study book.

**LEADING A GROUP?**

Each group member will need a *How Much More* Bible Study Book, which includes video access. Because all participants will have access to the video content, you can choose to watch the videos outside of your group meeting if desired. Or, if you're watching together and someone misses a group meeting, they'll have the flexibility to catch up! A DVD set is also available to purchase separately if desired.

Browse study formats, a free session sample, video clips, church promotional materials, and more at

**lifeway.com/howmuchmore**